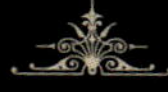

Ut Pictura Poesis

What Language to say The Arts?

French Rhetoric and German Aesthetics in the Eighteenth Century

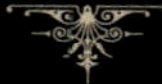

Prof. Marc Fumaroli
de l'Académie française

Translated by
Darius A. Spieth

Louisiana State University
School of Art

Baton Rouge, LA 70803

Published by Louisiana State University
School of Art

123 Art Building, Baton Rouge, LA 70803
Distributed by Louisiana State University Press
ISBN: 978-0-8071-6415-0

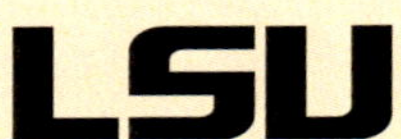

College of
Art + Design
School of Art

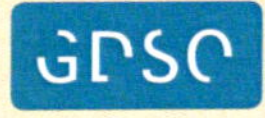

Design & Production

Project Director: Kitty Pherey
Creative Director: Luisa Restrepo
Faculty Advisors: Lynne Baggett & Rod Parker
Book Designer: Tina Korani
Production Artist: Gabe Hilliard

Photograph Credits: Santi Caleca: cover; The Philadelphia Museum of Art / Art Resource, NY: p. 13; Davis Museum at Wellesley College / Art Resource, NY: p. 12; © RMN-Grand Palais / Art Resource, NY: p. 15; Erich Lessing / Art Resource, NY: p. 14 & p. 23; Gianni Dagli Orti / The Art Archive at Art Resource, NY: p. 18 & p. 37; Album / Art Resource, NY: p. 25; © Vanni Archive/ Art Resource, NY: p. 32; © British Library Board / Robana / Art Resource, NY: p. 35; By kind permission of the Trustees of the Wallace Collection, London / Art Resource, NY: p. 41; Hervé Lewandowski, © RMN-Grand Palais / Art Resource, NY: p. 59; Heidelberg University Library, G 5769 B RES, p. I: p. 33; Darius A. Spieth: p. 19.

Acknowledgements

The historical relationship between Louisiana and France is, by definition, a special one. It began in 1682, when René-Robert Cavelier, Sieur de La Salle, led an expedition down the Mississippi River from the Great Lakes and named the Mississippi basin "La Louisiane" in honor of Louis XIV. French language and French culture are still at the heart of Louisiana today, and the region holds as much a particular fascination for many modern citizens of France as France holds for the citizens of Louisiana.

Marc Fumaroli, member of the Académie française, and a celebrated intellectual and writer on the subject of rhetorics—visual and literary—is one such modern citizen of France, and he took great pleasure in the many obvious connections with the culture of his homeland as he travelled in the region in the fall of 2013. His visit was occasioned by an invitation from the College of Art & Design at Louisiana State University to deliver a talk as part of that year's Paula G. Manship Endowed Lecture Series.

The School of Art's Visiting Artists and Scholars Program is closely aligned with the Manship Lecture Series, and both are integral to our mission to provide students vital, comprehensive experiences in the meaning, the history, and the practice of art and design. Every year we invite a diverse group of internationally recognized artists and scholars to present ideas and perspectives that will be useful to our students and to contribute to the intellectual and artistic life of the university and the community through lectures, workshops, seminars, class visits, and exhibitions.

Professor Darius Spieth, who led the initiative to bring Marc Fumaroli to LSU, notes in his preface

how the author's "cultural accomplishments are the product of a long maturing process, contemplation, and respect for traditions." The visit of such a seminal intellectual figure as Professor Fumaroli was itself the product of such a process, and it turned out to be a major event in Louisiana. A large number of people, on both sides of the Atlantic, contributed to making the visit both meaningful and rewarding for all involved.

In France, Cathérine Fabre and Pierre Berger of the Collège de France and Paul De Sinety, of the Institut Français in Paris, contributed both their enthusiasm and their material support to the project. Sébastien Fumaroli and Jean-Mathieu Robine provided considerable logistical assistance on the ground and with communications.

In New Orleans, Jean-Claude Brunet, Consul General, and Madame Brunet, ably assisted by Phillipe Aldon, Cultural Attaché of the Consulate General of France, threw themselves into planning and hosting several events, with support by Béatrice Germaine and Marie-Agnes Scialfa.

On the LSU campus, members of the faculty and administration of the College of Humanities and Social Sciences participated in the planning of the visit and were partners of the College of Art and Design in presenting the lecture. Greg Stone, Chair of the French Department and Boyd Professor Suzanne L. Marchand in the Department of History were early and invaluable supporters of the project, as was Professor Adelaide Russo, Director for the LSU Program in Comparative Literature. At Hill Memorial Library Jessica Lacher-Feldman, Head of Special Collections, and Leah Wood Jewett, Exhibitions Coordinator, curated a special exhibition celebrating Professor Fumaroli's lifetime accomplishments and hosted a reception in his honor.

Dean Alkis Tsolakis of the College of Art and Design was an early, immediate, and indefatigable supporter of the project, as was Tom Sofranko,

Associate Dean. Elizabeth Duffy, Lisa West, Vincent Cellucci, and Marshall Roy—staff members of the college—facilitated the resolution of numerous logistical, practical, and communication issues.

In the School of Art, Kitty Pheney, Director of New Initiatives, was on hand throughout the visit, smoothing the path, organizing the schedule, and generally guiding things along. Art History Graduate Students Brandi Batts, Alexandria Guillory, Kara Blanken, Lydia Dorsey, and Glauco Adorno all helped make these events exciting and meaningful for the LSU student population. Joe Givens, Director of the McNair Program at LSU organized a trip to Natchez, Mississippi, which was a particular delight for Marc Fumaroli since it made his groundbreaking scholarship on Chateaubriand—whose novel *Atala* is situated in Natchez—come alive.

As with many of the School of Art's community outreach activities, the members of the Glassell Gallery Group, as well as the many donors to the school's Annual Fund, provided invaluable support.

Finally, we would like to extend our gratitude to William Sawaya of Sawaya & Moroni, for allowing us to reproduce his artwork on the cover of this publication. His sensuous glass creations owe their inspiration to Charles Baudelaire's *Les Fleurs du Mal*, and thus epitomize the affinity of art and poetry—from both Horace's and Fumaroli's point of view.

On behalf of the School of Art, my colleagues, and our students, I extend my profound and heartfelt thanks to all these capable and enthusiastic people who came together to make possible the event, as well as this record of what was said.

Rod Parker
Director
LSU School of Art

Preface

Marc Fumaroli's Manship Lecture "*Ut Pictura Poesis*, or What Language to Say 'The Arts'" represented the culminating event of what the author pronounced, on the occasion of his fall 2013 visit at Louisiana State University, his "last of many travels to the United States." Without exaggeration, it can therefore be called a historical document. A member of the French Academy, an eminent scholar of rhetoric across the ages, and an insightful observer of literary and artistic life at the turn of the twenty-first century, Professor Fumaroli upholds the idea that creativity and erudition must exist outside the shifting tides of intellectual and technological fashions. Cultural accomplishments, for him, are the product of a long maturing process, contemplation, and respect for traditions, as opposed to mediated "buzz." Notions such as "quality," "skills," "craftsmanship" are still relevant criteria for looking at art and for finding beauty. Activities such as beholding a picture, reading poetry, or carrying on a conversation are examples of pleasures that can only be relished in a leisurely way and in a dialogical (but not dialectical) context. There is no shame in pleasure. Moreover, he is an advocate for the deacceleration of time, a slowing down to allow for engagement and reflection.

Professor Fumaroli's positions are not reactionary, however, for the simple reason that he rejects the rigors of any kind of doctrine. Rules, doctrines, and prescriptions prevent us from appreciating that which is meant to induce pleasure: the intuitive and sensuous absorption of a beautiful turn of phrase or the ingenious detail

in a painting. The modernity of his thought is obvious, for example, in his spirited defense of America's cultural values and innovative mind set, as for instance expressed in his book *Paris-New York and Back: A Travel in Arts and Images* (*Paris-New York et retour: Voyage dans les arts et dans les images*), which reproduced the pages of a diary kept, between 2007 and 2008, in both cities. Given that the notion of "cultural exceptionalism" has enjoyed, ever since the era of President Charles de Gaulle and his minister of culture, André Malraux, the status of something of an official state doctrine, such musings, by a member of the French Academy, almost amount to intellectual heresy. French "cultural exceptionalism," it must be recalled, can only function against the backdrop of her cultural other, America.

As will be obvious from the following pages, Professor Fumaroli is no friend of the term "aesthetics," which he sees as intrinsically tied to the rule of conceptualism in art. This rule, he argues, has asserted itself overtly over the last seventy or so years, but its roots are much older. From this premise, his essay reframes a fundamental question about the art of our time in a new and heretofore rarely explored context. Fumaroli casts into doubt the commonplace assumption that, sometime between World War I and the Counter Culture of the late 1960s, ideas, *for the first time*, began to supersede the hands-on making of art. In 1917, Marcel Duchamp submitted a pre-fabricated urinal to a juried art exhibition as a calculated provocation; half a century later, Pop art was blatantly imitating advertising and industrial production techniques in Warhol's serialized silkscreen prints. In between – and this is admittedly a large historical parenthesis, since it comprises the rise and fall of fascism and another world war – traditional forms of academic training for visual artists had all but vanished, and the notion that ideas mattered more than the actual crafting of an object had become common coin of the expanding definitions of art. Concurrently,

the myth of the artist as an individual creator-genius was demolished. Not only could anything be art, but now anybody could also be an artist.

Fumaroli reminds us, however, that the tyranny of the mind over these senses runs historically much deeper than the mid-years of the twentieth century, and takes us back to classical antiquity and controversies that emerged during the age of the Enlightenment. The "theoretical turn" has its ancestor in late eighteenth-century German figures like Johann Joachim Winckelmann or Anton Raphael Mengs, a scholar of classical antiquity and his painter-friend, who spent critical years of their careers in Rome. By 1750, excavations in southern Italy of the Roman cities of Pompeii and Herculaneum had unearthed a wealth of new information about daily life in antiquity and infused the study of classical civilizations with fresh energy. Winckelmann's attempt to systematize the study of the classical past, to match extant artworks and historical texts, to impose theoretical frameworks consisting of distinctions between "the high" and "the beautiful" style, and to develop models for the cyclical rise and fall of civilizations across history, were complemented by the more purely philosophical but equally theory-heavy writings of his contemporaries Gotthold Ephraim Lessing, Immanuel Kant, or the British scholar Edmund Burke. While in Rome, Winckelmann promoted the paintings of his friend Mengs as valid reincarnations of the classical past. For both men, beauty was not in the eye of the beholder, but could be defined, taught, had fixed qualities, and followed a canon. They also held nationalist prejudices against prior attempts to interpret antiquity from a French perspective that issued forth from the "grand siècle," when Louis XIV ruled. Under the reign of the "sun king," Versailles was built. The palace gave architectural form to France's artistic refinement and technical know-how, which were internationally unparalleled and universally admired. The prestige of the French language made it supersede Latin as the dominant

international *lingua franca*. Contemporary plays by Corneille and Racine or paintings by Nicolas Poussin and Claude Lorrain transported spectators back to an idealized classical world, whose luster and values now reflected back upon France's own "âge classique." This French classical tradition extended deep into the eighteenth century, up to the Revolution and beyond. During the last years of the Old Regime, for example, the great master of neoclassical painting, Jacques-Louis David, according to his biographer Étienne Delécluze, "knew but the titles and the engravings illustrating the writing of the antiquarian-philologists," while he "never took a liking to Mengs' talent."[1]

Several of the scholars Professor Fumaroli cites in defense of an appreciation of art based on poetry, as opposed to aesthetics, emerged from this cultural moment of the seventeenth century: Roger de Piles and Abbé Jean Baptiste Du Bos. Both stand in a rhetorical tradition that maintains the insufficiency of words to capture (let alone replace) the sensorial, and therefore sensual experience of art. In their rejection of theorizing art, they bridge the chronological gaps separating Aristotle in ancient Greece; Horace, Vitruvius, and Pliny the Elder in ancient Rome; and modern French thinkers and poets from the Enlightenment to the early twentieth century: Diderot, Amaury-Duval, Théophile Gautier, Baudelaire, and Paul Valéry. What connects their approaches across the ages is Horace's saying *Ut pictura poesis*, affirming the quintessential link between painting and poetry. In 1948, the famous art connoisseur Bernard Berenson wrote in *Seeing and Knowing* that "I am uneasy about this contradiction between looking and knowing, distressed over having to interpret everything we see beyond, as tangible objects in a familiar space. So I revel in the pictures of a van Eyck, or a Roger van der Weyden, [...] because they make me traverse space with no fatigue."[2] Many of today's viewers will experience a similar unease over so much contemporary art, whose comprehension is critically dependent upon the

enunciations of a touring global circus of experts that leave one, more often than not, baffled and confused. In the absence of visual intrigue, theoretical barriers make a lot of art unnecessarily aloof and, therefore, inaccessible – if not irrelevant – for all but the small coteries who know how to read the "codes" of the art world. Marc Fumaroli reminds us that the most compelling aspect of any artwork is always the intrinsic interest evoked by the tangible object itself.

Darius A. Spieth
Professor of Art History
Louisiana State University

Chapter 1

What Language to say The Arts?

French Rhetoric and German Aesthetics in the Eighteenth Century

Marc Fumaroli,
de l'Académie française.

Allow me to begin with an anecdote that I have myself witnessed, and which stands, in large part, at the origins of the reflections I would like to share with you tonight.

Some years ago, the Committee of Social Thought at the University of Chicago, where I taught for one semester per year, organized a colloquium on contemporary art. Among the critics invited were the major apologists of contemporary art. Arthur Danto, the famous philosopher and aesthetician, was obviously part of them. He is the author of such bestsellers as ***The Transfiguration of the Commonplace***, ***The End of Art***, and ***The Madonna of the Future: Essays in a Pluralistic Art World.***

In the vast neo-gothic lecture hall where the presentation took place, Danto entered like a guru with flowing white hair and a Mao collar.[3] One could have taken him, in the Paris of the 1930s, for an artist from Montmartre, rather than a philosophy professor of the Sorbonne.

Quel Langage pour dire Les Arts?

Rhétorique Française et Esthétique Allemande au XVIIIe Siècle

Marc Fumaroli,
de l'Académie française.

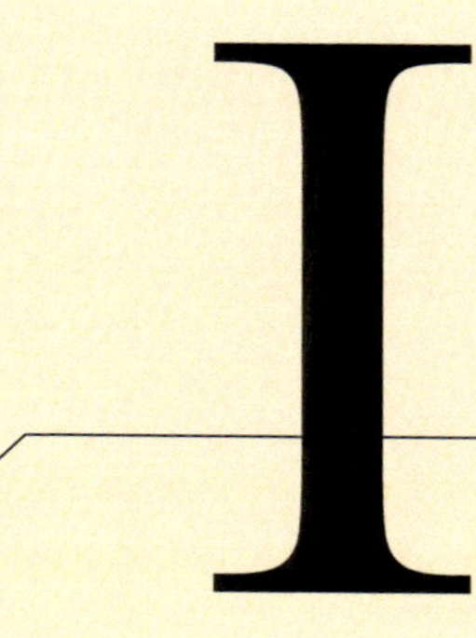

Permettez-moi de vous raconter, pour commencer, une anecdote vécue, et qui est pour une bonne part à l'origine des recherches que j'ai choisies de vous exposer aujourd'hui.

Il y a quelques années, le Committee for Social Thought de l'Université de Chicago, où j'enseignais pendant un semestre, organisa un colloque sur l'Art contemporain. Les critiques qui en faisaient l'apologie furent invités. Arthur Danto, le célèbre philosophe et esthéticien de Columbia fut évidemment de la partie. Il est l'auteur de best-sellers tels que ***La transfiguration du banal*** (trad. fr. 1981) ; ***La fin de l'Art*** (trad. fr. 1984) et la ***Madone du futur*** (trad. fr. 2003).

Dans la vaste salle néo-gothique où les communications étaient lues, on vit entrer un gourou à longs cheveux blancs et col Mao, qu'on aurait pris à Paris, dans les années 30, pour un artiste de Montmartre plutôt que pour un professeur de philosophie à la Sorbonne.

The moment of his talk having arrived, the Master spoke up and explained to us in Hegelian[4] terms the death of Art and the end of History; then, by taking a brilliant turn of dialectical reversal, he described the vast territory thus liberated for Art in the postmodern and post-historical age, in which we were fortunate enough to live.

In this era liberated from all straitjackets, Art prospers like never before in the ruins of the ancient art that preceded it. The new creativity of image makers (*plasticiens*) and their dealers, replacing the ancient artists, former patrons and persons of good taste (*amateurs*), found a natural leadership figure in Andy Warhol, like Michelangelo had been a leader for the Mannerists in Vasari's ***Lives***. While Michelangelo selected as his motto Horace's *Ut pictura poesis,*[5] Warhol multiplied – thanks to the magic wand of the contemporary – the *readymade* of Marcel Duchamp into so many three-dimensional masterworks, exhibited by galleries and museums in limited-edition series offered to consumption by an elite of billionaire collectors. The Brillo box,[6] for exam-

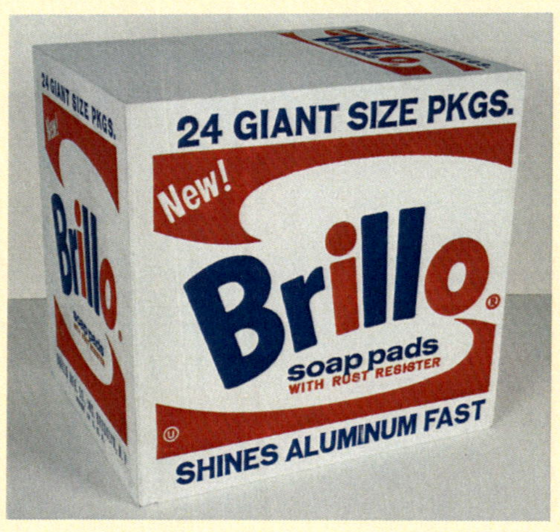

Andy Warhol, ***Brillo Box***, 1964, synthetic polymer paint and screenprint ink on wood, 17 in. x 17 in. x 14 in. (43.2 cm x 43.2 cm x 35.6 cm). Davis Museum, Wellesley College, Wellesley, MA. Museum purchase and partial gift of The Andy Warhol Foundation for the Visual Arts, Inc., 1993.25.

ple, in an instantaneous transformation of the banality of consumer society's artifacts, became the star of the Art market.

Donc, le Maître, à l'heure dite, prit la parole et nous expliqua en termes hégéliens la mort de l'Art et la fin de l'Histoire, puis par un brillant renversement dialectique, il décrivit l'immense territoire ainsi libéré pour l'Art de l'époque postmoderne et post-historique où nous avions la chance de vivre.

Dans cette ère libérée de tous les carcans, l'Art prospère comme jamais, dans les ruines des arts anciens. La nouvelle créativité de plasticiens, remplaçants les anciens artistes, a trouvé un chef de file idéal, comme Michel Ange l'avait été pour les maniéristes dans les ***Vies*** de Giorgio Vasari. Michel Ange avait pour devise l'***Ut pictura poesis*** d'Horace ; Andy Warhol a généralisé, grâce à la baguette magique contemporaine, le *ready made* de Marcel Duchamp, la transfiguration instantanée de la banalité des artefacts de la société de consommation (par exemple la boîte Brillo, star des supermarchés) en autant de chefs-d'œuvre en trois dimensions, exposés en série limitée, en galerie ou au musée et proposés à la consommation d'une élite de collectionneurs milliardaires.

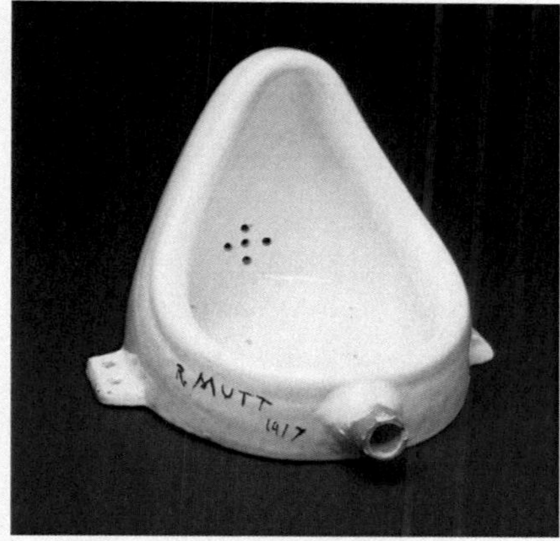

Marcel Duchamp, ***Fountain***, 1950 (replica of a 1917 original), porcelain urinal, 12 x 15 x 18 in. (30.5 x 38.1 x 45.7 cm). Philadelphia Museum of Art, Philadelphia. Gift (by exchange) of Mrs. Herbert Cameron Morris, 1998.

Quand le savant propos du Maître eut pris fin, ponctué d'applaudissements polis, je remarquai à ma droite un jeune couple d'une rare beauté et qui n'applaudissait pas. Le modérateur de la session fit l'appel rituel aux questions. Mon voisin se leva aussitôt, demandant la parole d'un geste de la main, et par son autorité naturelle, attirant

Once the erudite words of the Master, punctuated by polite applause, had come to an end, I noticed to my right a young couple of a rare beauty that did not applaud. The moderator of the session called for the ritual question and answer period. My neighbor got up immediately and, with a hand gesture, demanded to speak; by virtue of his natural authority, he attracted the attention of everybody in the room: "Dear professor, I am a poet, not a philosopher as you are, and I do not understand your reduction of Art to its own concept and its dependence upon 'the last stage of the discursive debate' inside what you called the actual 'art world.' As a poet, I prefer artworks to their concept, if there are any, and I do only consult, in order to enjoy them or not, my own sentiment and not at all the last conceptual trend prevailing in the 'art world.'"

Having finished, he sat down again next to his splendid companion. Professor Danto was obviously not used to being contested. He allowed himself some moments of silence, then, turning to his challenger, he exclaimed: "You confound two different things, one is my public task as an authority in philosophy and as an expert in aesthetics, to determine the importance or the insignificance, of such and such artist, such and such installation or performance, in such and such gallery, along the actual Art context and contest. But I am also a private person, with his personal taste, and I can assure you that in this capacity, I prefer by far... Chardin!"[7]

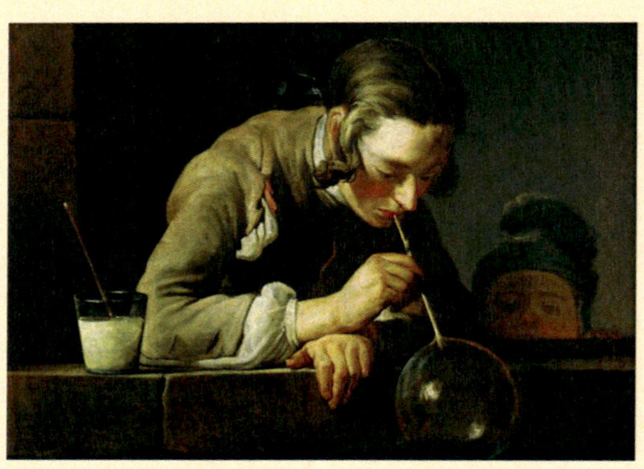

Jean-Baptiste Simeon Chardin, ***Blowing Soap-Bubbles*** (***Les Bulles de savon***), after 1739, oil on canvas, 23 5/8 x 28 3/4 in. (60 x 73 cm). Los Angeles County Museum of Art, Los Angeles. Gift of The Ahmanson Foundation, M.79.251.

l'attention de toute la salle : « Dear professor, I am a poet, not a philosopher as you are, and I do not understand your reduction of Art to its own concept and its dependence upon "the last stage of the discursive debate" inside what you called the actual "art world". As a poet, I prefer artworks to their concept, if there are any, and I do only consult, in order to enjoy them or not, my own sentiment and not at all the last conceptual trend prevailing in the "art world"».

Et il se rassit auprès de sa splendide compagne. Le professeur Danto n'était pas manifestement accoutumé à la contestation. Il se ménagea quelques instants de silence, puis, se penchant du côté de son contradicteur, il s'écria : « You confound two different things, one is my public task as an authority in philosophy and as an expert in aesthetics, to determine the importance or the insignificance, of such and such artist, such and such installation or performance, in such and such gallery, along the actual Art context and contest. But I am also a private person, with his personal taste, and I can assure you that in this capacity, I prefer by far... Chardin ! »

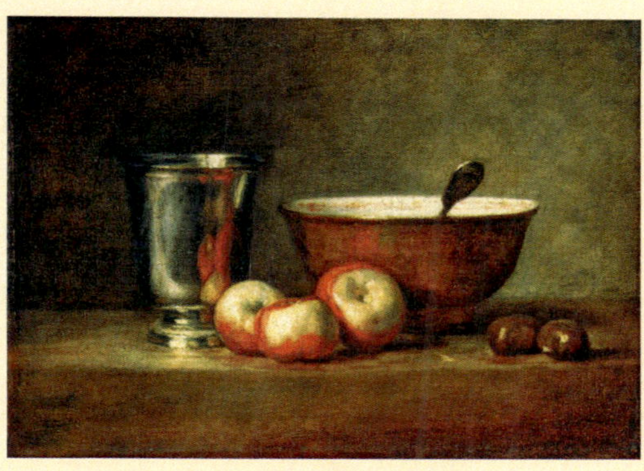

Jean-Baptiste Simeon Chardin, ***The Silver Goblet*** (***Le Gobelet d'argent***), ca. 1760, oil on canvas, 13 in. x 16 1/8 in. (33 x 41 cm). Louvre, Paris, MI 1042

De très grands et célèbres poètes français ont partagé le sentiment de mon voisin du colloque de Chicago. Théophile Gautier, en 1855, s'est montré sévère envers l'« Esthétique » à l'allemande, discipline philosophique profondément étrangère à la manière française d'aborder les questions artistiques, c'est-à-dire la critique d'art telle que

Very important and celebrated French poets have shared the sentiments of my neighbour from the Chicago colloquium. In 1855, Théophile Gautier showed himself severe towards German-style "Aesthetics," a philosophical discipline profoundly alien to the French approach to artistic questions, or the way in which Gautier thought of art criticism. The metaphysical discourse about the arts that German aestheticians hold legitimate engendered, according to the poet, a certain form of art, philosophical in itself, which he qualified as "aesthetics of art" and about which he said: "Germany indulges itself in the aesthetics of art. In this country, people do not paint, they write ideas."

During the same time, Baudelaire showed his support for Gautier, whom he greatly admired, dedicating, in 1861, his collected poems ***Les Fleurs du mal*** to him. The periodical ***L'Art romantique*** published, under the title "L'Art philosophique," excerpts from the unpublished papers left after the author's death, which contained a violent diatribe of the poet of the ***Phares*** against German aesthetics and outlined their consequences for the arts. Baudelaire asked:

"What is philosophical art according to the Germanic school of thought? It is a visual art that pretends to replace the book, which is to say to strike up a rivalry with the printing press so as to teach history, morals, and philosophy." Baudelaire meant to denounce in this manner what today's poet Yves Bonnefoy calls "conceptual thought," which, when applied to the arts, arrests them in their development and impoverishes them of the suggestive magic capable of yielding, in the words of Mallarmé, "rewards making up for the defaults of languages."

Reason and the faculty of drawing conclusions, which belong to the realm of the book and the written word, sterilize and desiccate the arts, while making them loose "their proper

Gautier la pratiquait. Le discours métaphysique sur les arts que tiennent les esthéticiens allemands légitime et engendre, selon le poète, une certaine forme d'art, elle aussi philosophique, qu'il qualifie d'« esthétique de l'art » et dont il dit : « L'Allemagne semble se complaire dans l'esthétique de l'art, Elle ne peint pas, elle écrit l'idée ».

Dans les mêmes années, Baudelaire se montrait solidaire de Gautier, dont il était un grand admirateur et à qui il a dédié ***Les Fleurs du mal*** en 1861. La revue ***L'Art romantique*** publia, tirée de ses papiers posthumes, et sous le titre ***L'Art philosophique***, une violente diatribe du poète des ***Phares*** contre l'esthétique allemande et ses effets sur les arts :

« Qu'est-ce que l'art philosophique, suivant la conception de l'école allemande ? demande Baudelaire. C'est un art plastique qui a la prétention de remplacer le livre, c'est-à-dire de rivaliser avec l'imprimerie pour enseigner l'histoire, la morale et la philosophie ». Baudelaire entend par là dénoncer ce que le poète d'aujourd'hui Yves Bonnefoy, appelle «la pensée conceptuelle » laquelle appliquée aux arts, les fige et les atrophie de la magie suggestive qui peut faire d'eux, selon le mot de Mallarmé, les « rémunérateurs du défaut des langues ».

Le raisonnement, la déduction qui appartiennent au livre et à l'écrit, stérilisent et dessèchent les arts en même temps qu'ils leur font perdre « leur vocation propre de sentiment et de rêverie ». Et Baudelaire ajoute, véritable prophète de la situation chaotique des arts aujourd'hui :

« Est-ce une fatalité des décadences, interroge le poète, qu'aujourd'hui chaque art manifeste l'envie d'empiéter sur l'art voisin, et que les peintres introduisent des gammes musicales dans la peinture, les sculpteurs, de la couleur dans la sculpture, les littérateurs des moyens plastiques dans la littérature, et d'autres artistes, ceux dont nous avons à nous

vocation for sentiment and reverie." And, like a true prophet of the chaotic situation of the arts today, Baudelaire added:

"Is it an inevitability of today's decadent situation that every art form longs to intrude on the territory of its neighbor: that painters introduce musical scales to painting; sculptors apply color to three-dimensional work; writers use visual means in literature; while other artists, who preoccupy us presently, impose a sort of encyclopedic philosophy onto the visual arts themselves?"

Therefore, one can speak of a true tradition of modern French poets – all of them mindful of the arts and exceptional art critics themselves – ranging from Gautier yesterday to Bonnefoy today, while passing through Baudelaire and Verlaine, who came to reject the Germanic philosophy of aesthetics, a legacy of Baumgarten and Kant. This legacy would become the mother of the conceptual art that rules today over the market.

Paul Valéry, a marvelous exegete of the proper vocation of every member in the family of the visual arts – architecture, dance, painting, and drawing – inserts himself naturally in this tradition. As an art critic, he wrote some of the most profound pages ever dedicated to Corot,

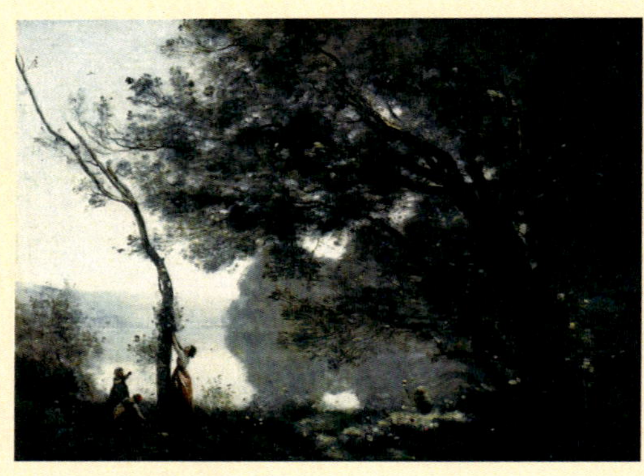

Camille Corot, ***Souvenir de Mortefontaine***, ca. 1864, oil on canvas, 25 1/2 in. X 35 in. (65 x 89 cm). Louvre, Paris, MI692bis.

Manet, and Degas.[8] Significantly, he began his essay "Around Corot" by stating that when

occuper aujourd'hui une sorte de philosophie encyclopédique dans l'art plastique lui-même ! »

Il y a donc une véritable tradition moderne des poètes français, tous très attentifs aux arts et tous exceptionnels critiques d'art, de Gautier à Bonnefoy en passant par Baudelaire et Verlaine, à repousser la philosophie allemande de l'Esthétique, héritière de Baumgarten et de Kant et mère de l'Art conceptuel qui règne aujourd'hui sur le marché.

Dans cette tradition, s'inscrit tout naturellement Paul Valéry, merveilleux exégète de la vocation propre à chacun des arts visuels, architecture, danse, peinture, dessin. Critique d'art, il a écrit les pages les plus pénétrantes que l'on ait consacrées à Corot, à Manet, à Degas. Dans son essai « Autour de Corot », il commence par dire : « On doit toujours s'excuser de parler peinture » (Pléiade, t. II, p. 1307).

En 1937, Valéry accepte de présider, en marge de l'Exposition universelle parisienne [à laquelle il a collaboré en écrivant les fameuses inscriptions du palais de Chaillot], un Congrès mondial des professeurs d'Esthétique.

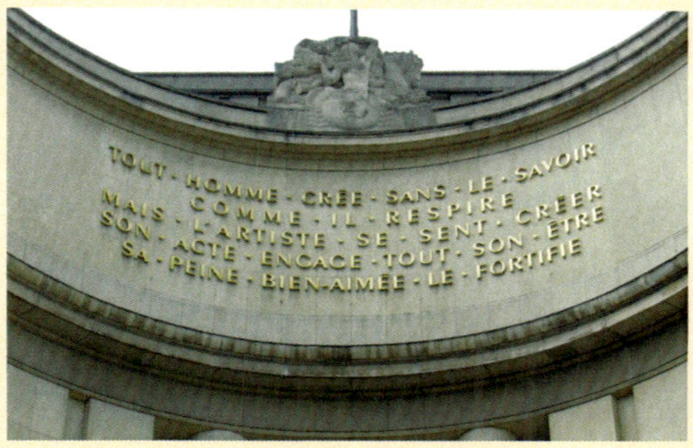

Façade of the Palais de Chaillot, Paris, with Paul Valéry's inscription reading: "Any man creates without knowing/like he breathes/But the artist feels compelled to create/His act becomes part of all his being/His labor of love fortifies him."

Dans son discours inaugural, Valéry, avec une parfaite courtoisie, se livre à une satire assez vive de l'Esthétique, extension aux arts de la philosophie de la connaissance inventée en Angleterre et en Allemagne, au cours du XVIIIe siècle.

speaking of this artist, "one must always apologize for talking about painting." (*Autour de Corot*, English tr. David Paul, in *Collected Works of Paul Valéry*, vol. XII, p. 134).

In 1937, in a collateral event of the Parisian World Fair, Valéry accepted to preside over the World Congress of Professors of Aesthetics. On the same occasion, he also contributed the famous inscriptions on the Palais de Chaillot in Paris.[9] In his inaugural speech, Valéry, with perfect politeness, took the liberty to develop a vivid satire of aesthetics, extension of the philosophical arts of knowledge invented in Great Britain and in Germany over the course of the eighteenth century. He said:

"What could have been more worthy of our philosopher's will to power[10] than this order of phenomena in which to *feel*, to *possess*, to *will*, and to *make* seemed to be joined in an essential and highly remarkable interaction that defied his Scholastic, not to say Cartesian,[11] efforts to split up the difficulty." (*Discours sur l'esthétique*, 1937; English tr. Herbert Read, in *Collected Works of Paul Valéry*, vol. XIII, p. 47)

The contrast is large between the human phenomena of the conception and the reception of a work of art; the former is synthetic and the least open to analysis, the latter susceptible to abstraction and to a philosophical appetite, which loves to take hold of the creative process in order to subject it to analysis and conceptualization through theory and metaphysical philosophy. "This kind of pleasure," insists Valéry, "is inseparable from developments that go beyond the sensibility and connect with the kinds of modified feeling which are prolonged and enriched in the channels of the intellect and sometimes lead to outward actions – on matter, on the senses, and on the minds of others – requiring the *combined exercise of all human powers*." (English tr. Herbert Read, vol. XIII, p. 46; my emphasis)

« Rien, dit-il, de plus digne de la volonté de puissance du Philosophe que cet ordre de faits [le plaisir que suscite l'œuvre d'art, excitant l'intelligence et incitant à l'imitation] dans lequel il trouvait le *sentir*, le *saisir*, le *vouloir* et le *faire*, liés d'une liaison essentielle, qui accusait une réciprocité remarquable entre ces termes, et s'opposait à l'effort scolastique, sinon cartésien, de division de la difficulté » (t. I, 1987, p. 1299).

Le contraste est grand entre le phénomène humain de la conception et de la réception de l'œuvre d'art, le plus synthétique et le moins susceptible d'analyse et d'abstraction, et l'appétit philosophique qui se plaît à s'en emparer pour le soumettre à l'analyse et à la conceptualisation de la théorie et de la métaphysique philosophique. « Cette sorte de plaisir, insiste Valéry, est indivisible de développements qui excèdent le domaine de la sensibilité, et la rattachent toujours à la production de modifications affectives, de celles qui se prolongent et s'enrichissent dans les voies de l'intellect et qui condouisent parfois à l'entreprise d'actions extérieures sur la matière, sur les sens et sur l'esprit d'autrui, exigeant *l'exercice combiné de toutes les puissances humaines* ». (je souligne, p. 1298-1299)

Néanmoins la volonté de puissance philosophique n'a pu résister à la tentation de coloniser ce domaine qui la défie. « Devant le mystère du plaisir dont je parle, écrit Valéry, le Philosophe justement soucieux de lui trouver une place catégorique, un sens universel, une fonction intelligible ; séduit, mais intrigué par la combinaison de volupté, de fécondité, et *d'une énergie assez comparable à celle qui se dégage de l'amour*, qu'il y découvrait ; ne pouvant séparer, dans ce nouvel objet de son regard, la nécessité de l'arbitraire, la contemplation de l'action, ni la matière de l'esprit, — toutefois ne laissa pas de vouloir réduire par ses moyens ordinaires d'exhaustion et de division progressive, ce monstre de la Fable Intellectuelle, sphinx ou griffon [...] en qui la sensation, l'action, le songe, l'instinct, les

Nevertheless, the philosophical will to power could not resist the temptation to colonize this domain, which poses a constant challenge. "In the presence of that mysterious pleasure of which I am speaking," writes Valéry, "the philosopher, justly concerned with giving it a categorical place, a universal meaning, an intelligible function; fascinated by, yet curious about the combination he has found here of sensuality, fecundity, and an *energy quite comparable to that which springs from love*; unable in his new object of attention, to separate necessity from the arbitrary, contemplation from action, matter from mind – the philosopher, I say, kept trying to apply his usual methods of reduction by exhaustion and progressive division to this monster of the Fable of Intellect, the sphinx or griffin [...] in which sensation, action, dream, instinct, reflection, rhythm, and excess are as closely intermingled as chemical elements in living bodies, [making man] put into [art] every bit of his mind, time, determination, in short, his life." (English tr. Herbert Read, vol. XIII, p. 48)

The "mysterious pleasure," "the combination of sensuality, fecundity, and an energy quite comparable to that which springs from love," which Valéry attributed to both the invention and the reception of an artwork, can be linked to a famous aphorism by Lichtenberg, published posthumously at the beginning of the twentieth century: "There are very few things that we could know with all five senses at one time." Among the things that the great German humorist alludes to only summarily, one surmises two that scare away Philosophy – the act of love making and the notion of the masterwork. Lichtenberg could have thought about Flemish paintings, representing either a collection of pictures and curiosities, or a still life, or a Madonna and Child, crowned with fruits and flowers: the sense of sight affirms itself by awakening, concurrently by synecdoche[12] and flashbacks, where fragments stand for the whole – the sense of touch (silk cloth, linen,

réflexions, le rythme et la démesure se composent aussi intimement que les éléments chimiques dans les corps vivants, [et font produire à l'homme] tout ce qu'il peut dépenser d'esprit, de temps, d'obstination, et en somme, de vie. » (p. 1300)

Le « mystère de plaisir », « la combinaison de volupté, de fécondité et d'une énergie comparable à celle qui se dégage de l'amour », que Valéry attribue à l'invention comme à la réception des chefs d'œuvre de l'art, rejoignent le célèbre aphorisme de Lichtenberg, publié posthume au début du XXe siècle : « Il y a très peu de choses que nous puissions connaître par les cinq sens à la fois ». Parmi ces choses que le grand humoriste allemand n'évoque que par prétérition, il en faut deviner deux qui effarouchent la philosophie, l'acte d'amour et le chef d'œuvre de l'art. Lichtenberg pouvait songer aux tableaux flamands représentant soit un cabinet de peintures et de curiosités,

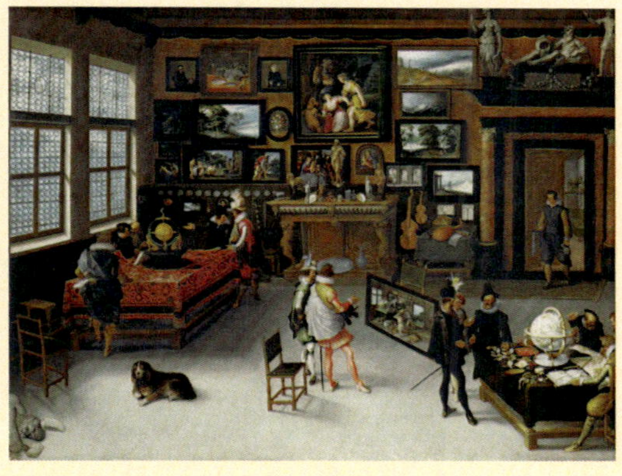

Adriaen van Stalbent, ***The Sciences and the Arts*** (***Les Sciences et les arts***), ca. 1650, oil on panel, 35 3/8 in. x 46 in. (89.9 cm x 117 cm). Museo del Prado, Madrid, P01405

soit un *still life*, soit une Madone à l'enfant couronnée de fruits et de fleurs : le sens de la vue s'y affirme en éveillant à la fois, par synecdoque et ricochet, parties pour le tout, le sens du toucher (les soieries, le linge, les chairs), celui du goût (les fruits, les liqueurs), celui de l'ouïe (les instruments de musique), et celui de l'odorat (les fleurs). Cette synthèse des cinq sens métaphorise à la fois l'indicible joie, voluptueuse de prime abord, que nous fait éprouver leur représentation picturale et le non moins indicible vertige de vanité et de

skin), that of taste (fruits, liquors), that of sound (musical instruments), that of smell (flowers). The synthesis of the five senses metamorphosizes into both the unspeakable joy, voluptuous at first glance, of beholding a pictorial representation and the no-less unspeakable vertigo of vanity and closure (finitude) into which we get plunged when, upon taking a second look, we discover the ephemerality of all these pleasures …

After having expounded on "mysterious pleasure" and the aesthetic philosopher who wants to explain a similarly fascinating "mystery," Valéry deploys his irony in all its sharpness. According to him, the lively multi-facetedness, in and off itself incomprehensible, of the artistic phenomenon is as defiant to reduction to scholastic abstraction as is the act of love, even though it was forced by aesthetic philosophy to prostrate itself on the bed of Procrustes, before the instruments of conceptual analysis could be applied. "In this realm," says the poet, "the virtues of purity, universality, strictness and logic engendered a number of paradoxes, the most startling of which is this: the Aesthetics of the metaphysicians decreed a cleavage between the *Beautiful* and *beautiful things*!" (English tr. Herbert Read, vol. XIII, p. 49)

"I doubt," added Valéry, "whether sufficient attention has been paid to this astonishing consequence of a Metaphysical Aesthetics: by substituting an intellectual knowledge for the immediate and singular effect of phenomena and their specific resonance, it tends to absolve us from the experience of the *Beautiful* as encountered in the sensory world. Once the essence of beauty has been extracted, once its general formulas have been noted, and nature along with art has been exhausted, surmounted, replaced by principles whose implications can be derived with certainty – all the works and aspects that delighted us might just as well vanish, or at most continue to serve as provisional examples

finitude où nous plonge au second regard l'éphémère de tous ces plaisirs…

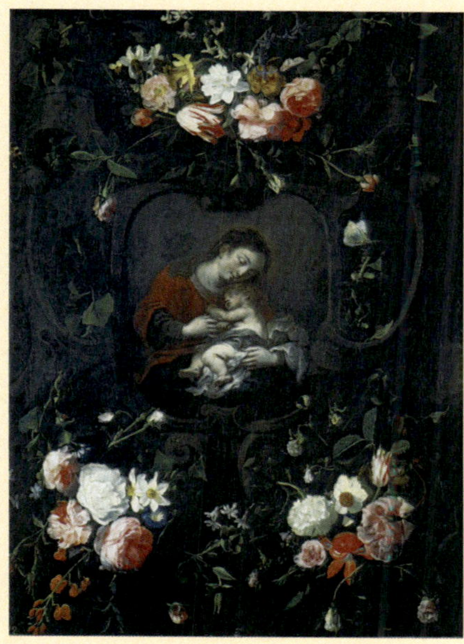

Daniel Seghers, ***The Vrigin and Child in a Garland of Flowers* (*Guirlande de fleurs avec Vierge et enfant*)**, 17th century, oil on canvas, 33 7/8 in. x 24 3/8 in. (86 x 62 cm). Museo del Prado, Madrid, NP 1905

Après avoir évoqué ce « mystère de plaisir » et le philosophe esthéticien qui veut expliquer un aussi fascinant « mystère », Valéry déploie toute l'acuité de son ironie. Selon lui, la polyédrie vivante, et comme telle insaisissable, du phénomène artistique, aussi peu réductible à l'abstraction scolastique que le sentiment et l'acte d'amour, a été contrainte par la philosophie esthétique à se coucher sur son lit de Procruste, avant d'exercer sur elle ses instruments d'analyse conceptuelle. « Pureté, dit le poète, généralité, rigueur, logique étaient en cette matière des vertus génératrices de paradoxes, dont voici le plus admirable : l'Esthétique des métaphysiciens exigeait que l'on séparât le *Beau* des *belles choses* ». (p. 1301)

« La déduction, ajoute-t-il, d'une Esthétique Métaphysique, qui tend à substituer une connaissance intellectuelle à l'effet immédiat et singulier des phénomènes et à leur résonance spécifique, tend à nous dispenser de l'expérience du *Beau*, en tant qu'il se rencontre dans l'expérience sensible. L'essence de la beauté

or teaching aids." (English tr. Herbert Read, vol. XIII, p. 59)

Half a century ahead of his time, Valéry foresaw the unsettling consequences of philosophical aesthetics, which diminish to their abstract dimension physical artistic practice and the experience of the beautiful alike, while favoring the philosophical concept of the idea of the Beautiful or judgments on matters of Beauty. In short, he had managed to diagnose, as early as 1937, the schizophrenia of an aesthetician as brilliant as Arthur Danto, delighted by the unexplainable "enigma" of Chardin's paintings unfolding before him, but feeling obliged, in his capacity as professional aesthetician with a reputation to defend in the contemporary art market, to legitimate its tenants. He did so even with respect to its most advertisement-like forms, for instance in the displacement of the common Brillo box from the supermarket to the rarefied and fashionable art gallery – an act sufficient to turn it into a work of art. All of these conceptual twists are self-sufficient, and they replace the absent work of art itself. The conceptualization of art does not go beyond the relabeling of the object to fit it into such-and-such a new category, infinitely more expensive, but without any value-added work performed in its transition from one place to another. The aesthetician who sanctions the legality of this transfer is perhaps the true "author" of the artwork; at least he has a better claim in this regard than the would-be artist who signed it.

Coming from the poet who wrote ***La jeune Parque***, this prescience of *readymades* and Pop Art, which are our contemporaries, comes as no surprise. Valéry is the scion of a long French tradition of resistance among artists, collectors, and art critics against a school of aesthetic thought that is primarily Germanic (Kant), and secondarily British (Burke). He also emerges as one of the most insightful interpreters of the French eighteenth century from his essays on

étant obtenue, ses formules générales écrites, la nature avec l'art épuisés, surmontés, remplacés par la possession du principe et par la certitude de ses développements, toutes les œuvres et tous les aspects qui nous ravissaient peuvent bien disparaître, ou ne plus servir que d'exemples, de moyens didactiques, provisoirement exhibés. »

Avec un demi-siècle d'avance, Valéry avait prévu les extrêmes conséquences d'une philosophie esthétique qui fait abstraction du métier comme de l'expérience du beau, au profit de concepts philosophiques de l'Idée du Beau ou du jugement sur le Beau. En somme il avait diagnostiqué, dès 1937, la schizophrénie d'un esthéticien aussi brillant qu'Arthur Danto, ravi par devers lui par « l'énigme » insondable des tableaux de Chardin, mais se tenant obligé, en tant qu'esthéticien de métier faisant autorité sur le marché de l'art contemporain, de légitimer des concepts – même les plus publicitaires, tel le déplacement de la commune boîte Brillo du supermarché à la rareté de la galerie d'art à la mode, ce qui suffit à faire d'elle une œuvre d'art. Tous ces concepts se suffisent à eux-mêmes, et ils tiennent lieu de l'œuvre d'art absente. Ils se contentent de la labéliser telle quelle dans cette autre catégorie, infiniment plus coûteuse, sans aucune valeur-travail ajoutée d'un lieu à un autre. L'esthéticien qui décide de la légalité de ce transfert est peut-être l'auteur de « l'œuvre », à meilleur droit que le prétendu artiste qui l'a signée.

De la part du poète de ***La jeune Parque***, cette prescience des *ready made* et du *Pop Art*, nos contemporains, ne doit pas nous surprendre. Valéry est l'héritier d'une longue tradition française de résistance des artistes, des amateurs et des critiques d'art à l'Esthétique allemande, et secondairement anglaise. Il est aussi l'un des interprètes les plus avertis du XVIIIe siècle français, dans ses essais sur Voltaire et sur Montesquieu. L'un et l'autre de ces auteurs ont été aussi des amateurs d'art, et ils ont farouchement opposé la pratique et l'expérience du goût à la théorisation

Voltaire and Montesquieu. Each one of these last two authors was also an art amateur, and both were adamant about separating the practice and the experience of taste from the theorization of the Beautiful. They followed the footsteps, in the eighteenth century, of the resistance mounted by poets and artists during the previous century against the empire of pedants and abstractions based on rules. This resistance by Corneille, Boileau, and Molière[13] found an echo in the eighteenth century, when even the philosophers of the ***Encyclopédie***[14] drew the line between, on the one hand, the intelligent and loving experience of art, and, on the other, British or German philosophy; between a sensual and an idealist approach; between an art that prefers to think itself rather than one that lets itself be felt. It is this French war of taste against the conceptualization of art by aestheticians, such as Burke and Kant, which dominated the age of Louis XV and Louis XVI, and which I would like to further investigate now.

du Beau. Ils ont pris le relais au XVIIIe siècle de la résistance opposée au siècle précédent, par les poètes et les artistes, à l'empire des pédants et à l'abstraction des règles. Cette résistance de Corneille, de Boileau, de Molière a trouvé des relais au XVIIIe siècle, où même les philosophes de l'***Encyclopédie*** opposent l'expérience intelligente et amoureuse des œuvres d'art à la philosophie anglaise ou allemande, sensualiste ou idéaliste, d'un Art qui préfère se penser lui-même au lieu de se faire sentir. C'est cette guerre française du goût contre la conceptualisation de l'Art par les esthéticiens tels que Burke et Kant, guerre qui occupe les règnes de Louis XV et de Louis XVI, que je voudrais maintenant évoquer.

Chapter 2

Since Greco-Roman antiquity the arts had to defend themselves against the philosophical logos, whose mission, in its final analysis, is iconoclastic. Plato chased the poets from his ***Republic***,[15] which seems to suggest that he would also have chased the artists. To defend themselves, the arts found a metalanguage of their convenience in the rhetoric and the poetics of Aristotle. This non-conceptual and non-dogmatic metalanguage – discursive but figurative, more turned towards practical ends than toward theory – gave them more points of reference and left them enough leeway to tinker at their craft (*bricolage*) with a greater degree of freedom and with greater enjoyment. Humanistic literature on art, like its sources in antiquity, borrowed its notions, structure, vocabulary, and its figures of speech from rhetoric, not philosophy. At the price of a mistranslation, this became the meaning of the saying *Ut pictura poesis,* which humanist authors of artistic literature extracted from Horace's ***Epistles to the Pisos***. And this is what, in the eighteenth century, the German

II

Les arts ont eu dès l'Antiquité gréco-romaine à se défendre contre le logos philosophique, dont la vocation en dernière analyse est iconoclaste. Platon chasse les poètes de sa République, ce qui laisse présager qu'il en chassera aussi les artistes. Pour se défendre, les arts ont trouvé un métalangage à leur convenance dans la rhétorique et la poétique d'Aristote. Ce métalangage non conceptuel, non dogmatique, discursif mais figuratif, plus tourné vers la pratique que vers la théorie, leur donnait assez de repères et leur laissait assez de jeu, pour œuvrer librement et avec bonheur à leur bricolage. La littérature d'art humaniste, comme ses sources antiques, a emprunté ses notions, ses schèmes, son vocabulaire, ses figures à la rhétorique, et non à la philosophie. Au prix d'un faux-sens, c'est ce que signifie l'apophtegme que cette littérature d'art extrait de l'***Épître aux Pisons*** d'Horace, *Ut pictura poesis*. Et c'est ce que ne voudra plus comprendre au XVIIIe siècle le philosophe allemand Lessing, dans son ***Laocoön***, publié en 1766.

philosopher Lessing did no longer want to understand when he published his ***Laocoön*** in 1766.[16]

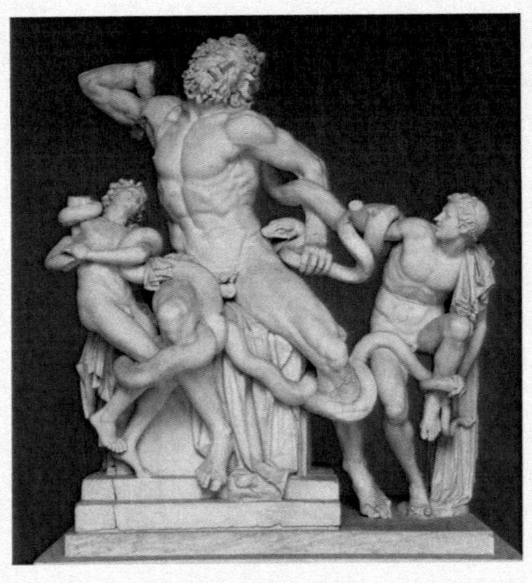

Athanadoros, Hagesandros and Polydoros of Rhodes, ***Laocoön and His Sons***, 1st century CE copy of an Hellenistic bronze original from the 2nd century BCE, marble, 7' 10 in. high. Musei Vaticani, Rome.

Horace's mnemotechnical apothegm[17] established the parallel between, if not the complementarity of, the two arts of imitation, painting and poetry, under a rhetorical regime. By different means, silent painting and the word, poetic and eloquent, engage in the same activity called *ekphrasis*,[18] in Latin *descriptio*. Both are called upon to transfix the soul of the spectator and the listener by the *energéia-evidentia* of their description and by the profundity of the images' imprint on the mind.

The literature of art was created, read, and commented, until the end of the sixteenth century, by artists from Cennino Cennini to Alberti, Vasari, and Lomazzo. This was also the case in classical antiquity, but many treatises by Greek artists mentioned by Pliny the Younger have disappeared, and modern authors of art treatises, in the final analysis, but sought to repair this loss and to fill the void left in modern archives and libraries.

The only classical art treatise that has survived quasi intact is ***De Architectura*** by the Roman author Vitruvius, a contemporary

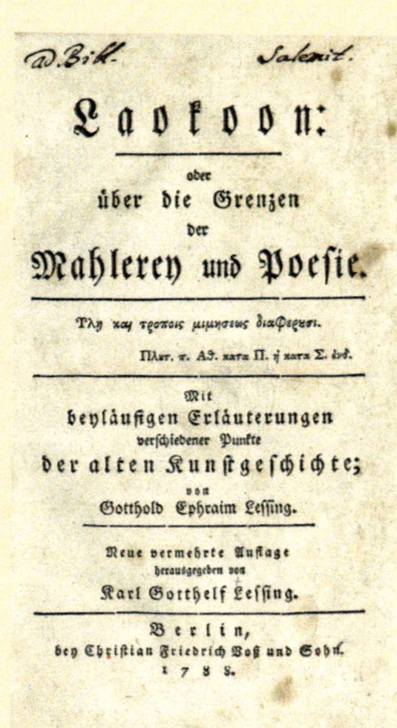

Laokoon:

oder

über die Grenzen

der

Mahlerey und Poesie.

Υλη και τροποις μιμησεως διαφερουσι.

Πλουτ. π. Αθ. κατα Π. ἢ κατα Σ. ἐνδ.

Mit

beyläufigen Erläuterungen

verschiedener Punkte

der alten Kunstgeschichte;

von

Gotthold Ephraim Lessing.

Neue vermehrte Auflage

herausgegeben von

Karl Gotthelf Lessing.

Berlin,

bey Christian Friedrich Voß und Sohn.

1788.

Gotthold Ephraim Lessing, *Laocoön*, cover page, 1788 edition.

Cet apophtegme mnémotechnique sanctionnait le parallèle, voire la complémentarité des deux arts d'imitation en régime rhétorique. Par des moyens différents, la peinture muette et la parole poétique et éloquente pratiquent la figure dite *ekphrasis*, en latin *descriptio*. Toutes deux sont à même d'attacher l'âme du spectateur et de l'auditeur par l'*energéïa-evidentia* de leurs descriptions et par le relief qui imprime les images dans l'esprit.

La littérature d'art, depuis Cennino Cennini jusqu'à Alberti, Vasari et Lomazzo, a été pratiquée, jusqu'à la fin du XVIe siècle, par des artistes. C'était le cas dans l'Antiquité, mais les nombreux traités d'artistes grecs mentionnés par Pline l'Ancien ont tous disparu, et les auteurs modernes de traités sur l'art cherchent, en fin de compte, à réparer cette perte et à combler le vide qu'elle a laissé dans les bibliothèques et les ateliers modernes.

Le seul traité antique d'art qui ait survécu quasi intact est le ***De Architectura*** du Romain Vitruve, un contemporain d'Horace qui dédie son livre à l'empereur Auguste. Il a pu et dû consulter les traités d'architectes grecs, mais il fait état, en praticien plus qu'en théoricien, d'une expérience proprement romaine.

of Horace, who dedicated his book to Emperor Augustus. He would have had the opportunity to consult the treatises by Greek architects since lost and indeed must have done so; but as a maker rather than as a theoretician, he foregrounds his strictly Roman outlook.

Another survivor from the ruins of the libraries of antiquity is the books XXXV to XXVI of the ***Natural History*** by Pliny the Older, father figure and model of the humanist antiquarian. Pliny does not attempt to theorize; he remains close to the rhetorical and poetic discourse that Greek artists used; he wrote an oral history based on the recollections transmitted from master to master in the workshops; he described summarily great masterworks; he recorded the customary anecdotes, which opened, as did Vasari with his ***Lives***, a vast field of discussion topics and provided a nurturing environment – as much for the creativity of artists as for the reception of their artworks by collectors.

In the tradition of Homer's *ekphrasis* of the Shield of Achilles,[19] one finds, on the dividing line between silent painting-poetry and eloquent poetry-painting, the collected descriptions of artworks by two Greek authors, Philostratus and Callistratus, sophists but not artists active during the third century, whose works have escaped destruction. These classical prose poems inspired, in Giambattista Marino's Italy and Félibien's or Fénelon's France, descriptive art criticism, in which Diderot, Gautier, and the Goncourts brothers excelled during the eighteenth and nineteenth centuries.[20]

Papal Rome, at the beginning of the seventeenth century, asserted itself as the iconophile capital of the arts.[21] It was here that the discursive privilege of artists, purveyors till then of both the making and theorizing of art, was extended to *virtuosi*, amateurs, collectors, antiquarians, connoisseurs, and friends of artists.

Autre survivant de la ruine des bibliothèques antiques, les livres XXXV-XXVI de ***L'Histoire naturelle*** de Pline l'Ancien, père et modèle de l'antiquariat humaniste. Pline ne prétend pas théoriser, il reste au plus près du discours rhétorique et poétique dont se servaient les artistes grecs, il répertorie la mémoire des maîtres qui se transmettaient dans les ateliers, il décrit sommairement les chefs-d'œuvre, il rapporte des anecdotes typiques, qui transmettent, comme le fera Vasari dans ses ***Vies***, une topique fertile, un milieu nutritif, tant pour l'invention des artistes que pour la réception de leurs œuvres par les *amateurs*.

Sur la frontière entre la peinture poésie muette et la poésie peinture parlante, où se situait déjà l'ecphrasis homérique du bouclier d'Achille, les recueils grecs de descriptions

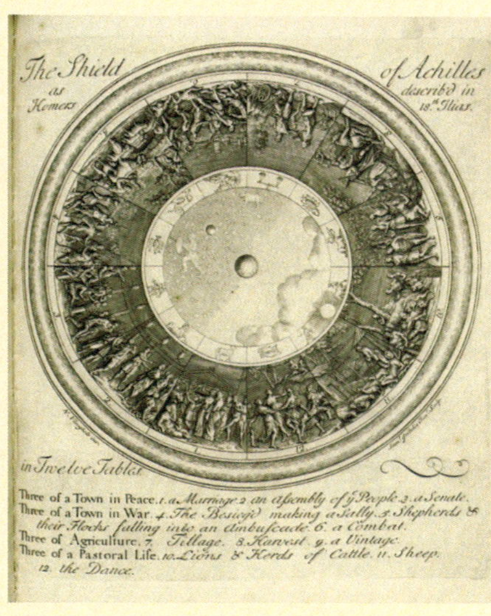

The Shield of Achilles as Described in Homer's ***Iliad***, 1715-1720, engraving, from: ***The Iliad of Homer***, translated by Mr Pope. British Library, London.

d'œuvres d'art, œuvres des deux Philostrate et de Callistrate, sophistes et non artistes du IIIe siècle, ont eux aussi échappé à la destruction. Ces antiques poèmes en prose amorcent, dans l'Italie de Giambattista Marino et dans la France de Félibien et de Fénelon, la critique d'art descriptive où excelleront au XVIIIe, puis au XIXe siècle, Diderot, Gautier, les Goncourt.

Au début du XVIIe siècle, dans la Rome des Papes, qui s'impose alors comme la capitale

These groups formed among themselves an art public – a public of privileged experts for sure, but nevertheless an enlarged public. A typical but by no means isolated example of these pursuits is Giulio Mancini's ***Considerations on Paintings*** (***Considerazioni sulla pittura***), which, during the 1620s, the future physician of Pope Urban VIII brought in circulation as a manuscript. These *Considerations* contained, besides a guide to good taste in matters of painting, a prescriptive monograph on the perfect virtuoso, the ideal interlocutor[22] of artists. As representatives of the following generation, the Fréart brothers introduced to the Parisian setting and to the framework of French institutions the Roman model of the *intenditore d'arte*,[23] who lends his ear to artists, is familiar with their workshops, and who has insider knowledge about their objectives, their language, and their profession. Nicolas Poussin[24] took on the role, in Rome or in his correspondence, of not only the teacher of his own art to young painters (Charles Le Brun, Charles Errard, Sébastien Bourdon, Gérard Dughet, …), but also that of an educator of French *virtuosi* and *intenditori*. The latter were his principal clients, whom he turned, by virtue of their acquiring specialized knowledge, into worthy collectors of his own artworks. From among this group, he taught the art writers Giovanni Pietro Bellori (1613-1696), a native Roman, and André Félibien, a Parisian, the principals which he had extracted from his long experience as a French painter active in both Rome and Paris.

Two generations later, a pair of French *intenditori d'arte* will rise to a very high public rank. One after the other, they will assume the position of true arbiters of good taste in the arts. Both joined one of the new Royal Academies founded by Colbert, where, in principle, the best artists and writers of the kingdom came together with the mission to provide guidance on the best style for the royal arts and letters. The sessions

iconophile des arts, le privilège des artistes, jusqu'alors les principaux praticiens-théoriciens des arts, s'étend aux virtuosi, amateurs, collectionneurs, antiquaires, connaisseurs, amis des artistes, qui forment avec eux et autour d'eux le public des arts, public d'experts privilégiés, mais public élargi. Typique, mais non isolé, le futur médecin du pape Urbain VIII, Giulio Mancini, fait circuler en manuscrit, dans les années 1620, ses ***Considerazioni sulla pittura***. Ces considérations constituent, outre un traité du bon goût en matière de peinture, une monographie prescriptive sur le parfait virtuoso, l'interlocuteur idéal des artistes. À la génération suivante, les frères Fréart transposent et transposent, à Paris, dans le cadre institutionnel français, le modèle romain de l'*intenditore d'arte*, à l'écoute des artistes, familier de leurs ateliers, et initié à leurs intentions, à leur langage, à leur métier. Nicolas Poussin aura été, à Rome ou par correspondance,

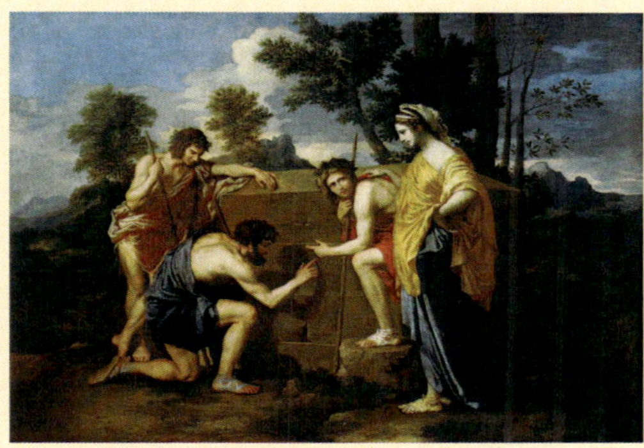

Nicolas Poussin, ***Shepherds of Arcadia*** (***Les Bergers d'Arcadie***), also known as ***Et in Arcadia Ego***, ca. 1638-1640, oil on canvas, 33 1/2 in. x 47 3/4 in. (85 x 121 cm). Louvre, Paris, INV7300.

non seulement un professeur de son propre art pour jeunes peintres (Charles Le Brun, Charles Errard, Sébastien Bourdon, Gérard Dughet...), mais un éducateur de *virtuosi* et d'*intenditori* français, ses principaux clients, qu'il rend dignes de collectionner, en connaissance de cause, ses propres œuvres. Parmi eux, il forme des écrivains d'art, un Romain, Giovanni Pietro Bellori (1613-1696), et un Parisien, André Félibien (1619-1695), selon les maximes qu'il avait lui-

of the Academy of Painting and Sculpture, the proceedings of which have now been published in their entirety, respected the privilege conceded to artists to speak to their experience and to the knowledge of their specialty. However, the academy's statutes provided that art *amateurs*,[25] who were treated as if they were initiated to the practice of art, be admitted on an equal basis as prime witnesses of artistic activities, as conversation partners, and as critics.

Roger de Piles (1635-1709), at the end of the seventeenth century, fulfilled in Paris the same role that, at the beginning of the century, Giulio Mancini had held in Rome: the archetype of one of those *amateurs* who were co-opted by the artists. Painter, engraver, diplomat, ingenious theoretician and art historian, he single-handedly educated two generations of connoisseurs – first through his numerous publications and later through his lectures at the Academy of Painting and Sculpture, where he was admitted in 1699 as consultant *amateur*. The dissemination of his ideas was essential for the success of the taste for all things "Rococo," which, during the Regency of the Duc d'Orléans[26] and from a Parisian perspective, carried the day over Versailles' grandeur. De Piles was a source of inspiration for the banker Pierre Crozat (1661-1740), the artistic advisor of the Duc d'Orléans. The mansion of the amateur Crozat, heavily frequented by the "colorists"[27] among the painters, was built in 1704 on the rue de Richelieu, two blocks away from the Orléans Palace. Crozat turned it into the most amazing museum of paintings and sculptures ever assembled by a private collector. Following Crozat's invitation to live and to paint there, Antoine Watteau emerged from anonymity and was elected member of the Academy in 1717, after the death of Louis XIV.

The case of Abbé Jean Baptiste Du Bos (1670-1742) is a little bit different. He entered the French Academy triumphantly in 1719,

même tirées de sa longue expérience de peintre français à Rome, mais aussi à Paris.

Aux deux générations suivantes, on voit s'imposer successivement deux *intenditori d'arte* français de très haute stature. Ils assument tour à tour un véritable office de prescripteurs du bon goût dans les arts. L'un et l'autre sont entrés dans une des Académies royales créées par Colbert où sont réunie en principe les meilleurs artistes et les meilleurs écrivains du royaume, avec pour mission de servir de boussole au meilleur style approprié aux lettres et aux arts royaux. Les séances de l'Académie de peinture et sculpture, dont les procès verbaux sont maintenant publiés dans leur intégralité, préservent le privilège reconnu aux artistes de parler de leur art d'après leur expérience et en toute connaissance de cause. Elles admettent cependant que des amateurs, quasiment adoptés par les artistes comme initiés à la pratique des arts, soient leurs premiers témoins, interlocuteurs et critiques.

Roger de Piles (1635-1709) fut à Paris, à la fin du siècle, ce qu'avait été à Rome au début du siècle, Giulio Mancini, l'archétype de ces amateurs adoptés par les artistes. Peintre, graveur, diplomate, ingénieux théoricien et historien de l'art de peindre, il a formé lui-même, par ses nombreuses publications, puis par ses conférences à l'Académie de peinture et sculpture où il entra en 1699, au titre de conseiller amateur, les deux générations de connaisseurs. Ils assurèrent le succès du goût dit « rocaille », qui fit prévaloir sous la Régence du duc d'Orléans la grâce parisienne sur la grandeur de Versailles. De Piles fut l'inspirateur du banquier Pierre Crozat (1661-1740), conseiller artistique du duc d'Orléans. L'hôtel particulier de cet amateur, plébiscité par les artistes coloristes, s'éleva à partir de 1704 dans la rue de Richelieu, à deux pas du palais d'Orléans. Crozat en fit le plus fabuleux musée de tableaux et de dessins jamais réuni par un collectionneur privé. Pendant trente

immediately after the publication of his ***Critical Reflections on Poetry and Painting*** (***Réflexions critiques sur la poésie et la peinture***). Unlike de Piles, Pierre Jean Mariette, or the Count de Caylus, he was not a quasi-professional art amateur. But he was one of De Piles' most alert readers. His talents as a diplomat, his historical erudition, his profound rhetorical culture combined to make him the uncontested master of an artistic taste, which kept its distance from fashion. "He read a lot," insinuated Voltaire in ***The Century of Louis XIV*** (***Le Siècle de Louis XIV***), underscoring the extraordinary success of the work.

Taking a leaf out of the book of the Quarrel between the Ancients and the Moderns, Du Bos, an adept of the Pascalian distinction[28] between intellectual acuteness (*esprit de finesse*) and the spirit of geometry, diverted the world of the arts away from that of the empire of scientific and philosophical reasoning. The visual arts, like poetry [*ut pictura poesis*], have as their engine not the search for truth, but the convincing and emotionally charged imitation of nature; above all, human nature. The final objective of these arts of imitation and of representation is to give more or less complete satisfaction to "the necessity to be occupied and to escape boredom." In the final analysis, Du Bos sketches an anthropology of "distraction," upon which he erected a universe of arts and spectacles. Here again, the subtle Abbé takes his inspiration from Pascal, great theoretician of tedium; but what is more, from a Pascal who would have retained many things from Epicureanism.[29]

Du Bos likes to quote the ***Suave mari magno***[30] of the Epicurean poet Lucretius in order to make his point about the difference between the imitation of passions, source of delectations, and their unmitigated experience, which makes one cruelly suffer. He cites another Epicurean motto, taken form Virgil's second Bucolic, ***Trahit suam quemque voluptas***,[31] to underline

ans, ce fut le rendez-vous des artistes, des musiciens, des amateurs et des curieux d'art parisiens ou de passage à Paris. C'est là qu'Antoine Watteau, invité à résider et à peindre, en même temps qu'il est élu à l'Académie, sortit de l'anonymat, en 1717, après la mort de Louis XIV.

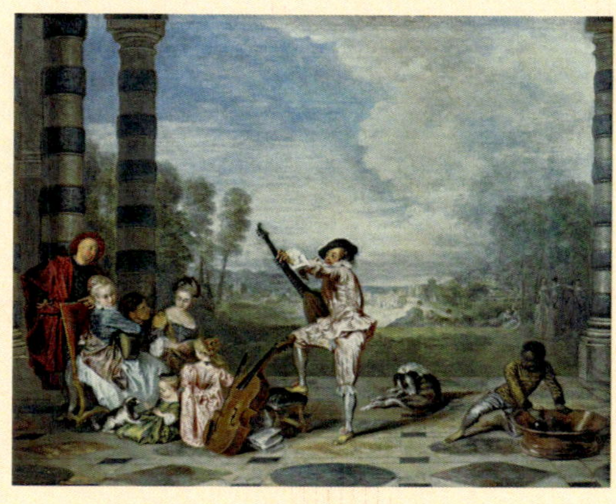

Antoine Watteau, ***The Music Party*** (***Les Charmes de la vie***), ca. 1718-1719, oil on canvas, 26 1/2 in. x 36 1/2 in. (67.3 x 92.5 cm). Wallace Collection, London, P410.

The setting of Watteau's *Les Charmes de la vie* can be identified as an actual scene from Pierre Crozat's country estate Montmorency.

Le cas de l'abbé Jean Baptiste Du Bos (1670-1742) est un peu différent. Il entra en triomphe à l'Académie française en 1719, immédiatement après la publication de ses ***Réflexions critiques sur la poésie et la peinture***. Il n'était pas comme un De Piles, un Pierre-Jean Mariette, ou un Caylus, un amateur d'art presque professionnel. Mais il fut le plus intelligent des lecteurs de De Piles. Ses talents de diplomate, son érudition historique, sa profonde culture rhétorique concoururent à faire de lui le maître incontesté d'un goût dans les arts qui sache garder ses distances avec la mode. « Il avait beaucoup lu », insinue Voltaire dans ***Le Siècle de Louis XIV***, tout en reconnaissant l'extraordinaire réussite de l'ouvrage.

Tirant les leçons de la Querelle des Anciens et des Modernes, Du Bos, adepte de la distinction pascalienne entre esprit de finesse et esprit de géométrie, soustrait le monde des arts à l'empire de la raison scientifique et philosophique. Les arts visuels, comme la poésie

how much the unlimited variety of human inclinations determines the extreme diversity of artistic forms.

This anthropology of leisure dispenses Du Bos from any metaphysical investigation of the Beautiful. In matters of taste, he strips pedants and geometric minds of their authority to pretentiously judge works of art according immutable rules, as opposed to the effect genuinely experienced by the audience. This approach also allows him to put himself in the place of the public, which knows very well if the painting, the poem, the play entertains or annoys. "Like in matters of cooking," writes Du Bos, "one savors the meal without knowing the rules, and one recognizes whether it is good or not."

"Innate in all of us," concludes Du Bos, "is a preordained aptitude to judge works that engage in the imitation of objects as found in nature." He calls it the "sixth sense," which does not need either rule or compass to make up its mind. Masterworks, and notably those of antiquity, emerge from the prolonged rallying over time of the "sixth sense." They serve as a touchstone to correct the premature and biased weeding out that fashion does in contemporary art. On election day for taste, the healthy innocence of ignoramuses is polled, while the pretentions of pedants are excluded. Molière, for one, first consulted his servant. While it is true that the consensus of ignorant people concerns but the work "in general," it fails to appreciate its "particular beauties." For this reason, they cannot have the last say. Moreover, Du Bos borrows from Cicero, Quintilian, and Vaugelas the doctrine of *sanior pars*,[32] pioneered by Roman conversationists – witnesses and arbiters, in the final analysis, of the good use of language and of the best *delectio verborum*.[33] Boileau, defending Homer against Perrault, contrasted the admiration for the Greek epic poet by the Prince of Condé, the Chancellor d'Aguesseau, and the Marshal de Turennes with the disdain of pedants and the difficulties of

[*ut pictura poesis*] ont pour principe moteur, non la recherche de la vérité, mais l'imitation vraisemblable et émouvante de la nature, et avant tout de la nature humaine. La cause finale de ces arts d'imitation et de représentation est de donner satisfaction, plus ou moins parfaitement, à la « la nécessité d'être occupé pour fuir l'ennui ». En fond de tableau Du Bos esquisse une anthropologie du « divertissement » qui fonde l'univers des arts et des spectacles. Là aussi, le subtil abbé s'inspire de Pascal, grand théoricien de l'ennui, mais d'un Pascal qui aurait beaucoup retenu de l'épicurisme. Du Bos cite volontiers le *Suave mari magno* du poète épicurien Lucrèce pour faire entendre la différence entre l'imitation des passions, source de délectation, et leur expérience directe, qui fait cruellement souffrir. Il invoque un autre apophtegme épicurien, prélevé sur la deuxième bucolique de Virgile, *Trahit suam quemque voluptas*, pour faire comprendre comment la variété illimitée des penchants humains détermine la variété extrême des formes d'art.

Cette anthropologie du loisir dispense Du Bos de toute métaphysique du Beau. Elle lui permet de priver d'autorité, en matière de goût, les pédants et les esprits géométriques qui prétendent juger les œuvres selon les règles immuables de l'art, et non selon l'effet réellement éprouvé par le public. Elle lui permet aussi de s'en remettre au sentiment du public, qui sait très bien si le tableau, le poème, la pièce de théâtre lui font plaisir ou l'ennuient. « Comme en matière de cuisine, écrit Du Bos, on goûte le ragoût sans savoir ses règles et on connaît s'il est bon ».

« Il est en nous tous, conclut Du Bos, un sens destiné pour juger de ces ouvrages qui consiste en l'imitation des objets touchants dans la nature ». Il l'appelle « le sixième sens », qui ne consulte ni la règle ni le compas pour se déterminer. Les chefs-d'œuvre, et notamment ceux des Anciens, sont l'objet, dans la longue durée, d'un plébiscite du « sixième sens ». Ils servent de

ignoramuses. Du Bos drew the outlines of a true "arts public," whose authority is stronger than the dictates of fashion. It is composed of "persons who have acquired insights, either through reading or by getting around in the world." "They are the only ones," he added, "who can rank poems and paintings, although such opinions on works excelling in beauty can also be found among the most common people when their emotions are stirred and they are asked to speak up." This aristocratic sociology of judging matters of taste concludes an anthropology of tedium, from which the arts emerge as a civilized form of therapy from ennui.

Du Bos elevated the opinion of the public, and not his proper reason, to the touchstone of good taste. He similarly failed to be a rationalist when he turned the focus of his discussion to the question of literary and artistic genius and to the times when this genius prospered. Science and philosophy are capable to compound progress, in linear time, while arts and letters, which speak to feeling and not reason, experience, over the course of their cyclical lifespan, but short bouts of increasing refinement, then attain rare peaks of perfection – the "Great Centuries (*Grands Siècles*)" – succeeded by decadence. At times of decadence, to prevent collapse or to escape it, it is important to affirm the mind set and the taste established during times of plenitude, exemplified by classical works destined to last for long periods. This attitude of resilience with respect to the torrents of time is the one adopted by Voltaire in ***The Century of Louis XIV*** (***Le Siècle de Louis XIV***); Du Bos borrowed it from the treatise ***On the Sublime*** by the Pseudo-Longinus, and Tacitus' ***Dialogue on Oratory***.

Writing under the rule of Louis XV that had just begun, Du Bos introduced an element of anxiety about decline and thus facilitated the onset of a deepening sense of nostalgia about the "Great Century," the *Grand siècle* –

pierre de touche pour corriger la comparaison trop hâtive et influencée par la mode entre œuvres contemporaines. Aux élections du goût, la saine innocence des ignorants participe, alors que les prétentions des pédants s'en excluent. Molière consultait d'abord sa servante. Il est vrai que l'approbation des ignorants porte sur l'œuvre « en général », et manque ses « beautés particulières ». Ils ne peuvent donc avoir le dernier mot. Aussi Du Bos reprend-il à Cicéron, à Quintilien, à Vaugelas, la doctrine de la *sanior pars* des locuteurs romains, témoins et juges en dernière analyse du bon usage de la langue, et de la meilleure *delectio verborum*. Boileau, pour défendre Homère contre Perrault, opposait l'admiration que portaient au poète épique grec le Prince de Condé, le Chancelier d'Aguesseau et le maréchal de Turenne, aux dédains des pédants et aux difficultés des ignorants (345). Du Bos dessine les contours du vrai « public des arts », dont l'autorité l'emporte sur l'intimidation des modes. Il est composé des « personnes qui ont acquis des lumières, soit par la lecture, soit par le commerce du monde ». « Elles sont les seules, ajoute-t-il, qui puissent marquer le rang des poèmes et des tableaux, quoi qu'il se rencontre dans les ouvrages excellents des beautés capables de se faire sentir au peuple du plus bas étage et de l'obliger à se récrier » (351). Cette sociologie aristocratique du jugement de goût vient ainsi compléter une anthropologie de l'ennui et des arts comme sa thérapeutique civilisée.

Du Bos fait du sentiment du public, et non de sa raison, la pierre de touche du bon goût. Il est tout aussi peu rationaliste quand il en vient au génie littéraire et artistique et aux époques où ce génie a prospéré. La science et la philosophie sont susceptibles de progrès cumulatifs, dans un temps linéaire, tandis que les arts et les lettres, qui s'adressent au sentiment, non au raisonnement, ne connaissent, dans leur temps cyclique, qu'un bref perfectionnement, conduisant à de rares pics de perfection, les

that of Louis XIV. This epoch was exclusively associated, in 1715, with the terrible political mistakes of the Sun King,[34] blanketing out that it provided a reliable benchmark for taste which contemporaries were only beginning to re-appreciate. Ever since 1719, Du Bos, whose writings anticipate Voltaire's ***Temple of Taste*** (***Le Temple du Goût***, 1733), called into question the "Rococo" style, which the previous generation of critics, clustered around De Piles, had embraced with enthusiasm as a reaction against the "Grand Taste," or "Grand Goût," of Versailles.

Nevertheless, neither Du Bos, nor Voltaire, accepted an instantaneous inevitability of decadence. They wanted to believe in the existence of an elite composed of persons with taste, which, enlightened by the ups and downs of history, is capable to short-circuit, by virtue of its natural authority, the temptations of barbarity or the "death of Art." In 1772, Voltaire, indulging in a kind of optimism so typical for the Enlightenment, still opined in the ***Supplement to the Questions of the Encyclopédie*** (***Supplément aux Questions sur l'Encyclopédie***):

"It is the persons of taste who govern in the long run the empire of the arts [...]. Eventually, the connoisseurs will carry with them the general public, and this is the only difference that exists between the most 'enlightened' nations and the most primitive ones, since the Parisian simpleton is in no way ahead of another vulgar person, but there exists in Paris a large enough number of cultivated spirits that can lead the crowds."

The great and wise author of these lines, a well-informed collector of his own age, would be inordinately surprised to discover how, in today's Paris, a FIAC art fair, framed by the most beautiful urban setting of the world, competes vainly and stupidly with the fairs in the star light of the global economy, like Art Basel, Frieze London, etc., instead of taking a counter-position.

« Grands siècles », bientôt suivis de décadence. Dans les temps de décadence, pour prévenir la disgrâce ou pour lui échapper, il faut garder l'esprit et le goût fixés sur les temps de grâce et sur les œuvres classiques qu'ils ont produits pour durer. Cette attitude de résistance au torrent des caprices est celle qu'adoptera le Voltaire du ***Siècle de Louis XIV*** ; Du Bos l'emprunte au traité ***Du Sublime*** du Pseudo-Longin et au ***Dialogue des orateurs*** de Tacite.

Il introduit ainsi, dans le règne de Louis XV qui commence, une anxiété de déclin et un début de nostalgie pour le Grand siècle, celui d'un Louis XIV dont on ne voulait connaître en 1715 que les terribles erreurs politiques, et dont on commence à apprécier la sûreté de goût. Dès 1719, anticipant sur ***Le Temple du goût*** de Voltaire (1733), Du Bos fait peser une ombre sur le goût « rocaille » que la génération précédente, formée par De Piles, avait embrassé avec transport, par fatigue du « Grand goût » de Versailles.

Il n'empêche que ni Du Bos, ni Voltaire ne cèdent à une fatalité immédiate de décadence. Ils veulent croire qu'une élite de gens de goût, éclairée par les vicissitudes historiques, est en mesure de couper court, par son autorité naturelle, aux tentations de barbarie ou de « mort de l'Art ». Avec un optimisme typique des Lumières, Voltaire peut encore écrire en 1772, dans le ***Supplément aux Questions sur l'Encyclopédie***:

« Ce sont les gens de goût qui gouvernent à la longue l'empire des arts [...]. Les connaisseurs seuls ramenèrent à la longue le public, et c'est la seule différence qui existe entre les nations les plus "éclairées" et les plus grossières, car le vulgaire de Paris n'a rien au dessus d'un autre vulgaire, mais il y a dans Paris un nombre assez considérable d'esprits cultivés pour mener la foule. »

Forgive me if I say that, from my point of view, this failure bestows honor to a capital and to a nation, which, for four centuries (if not for longer), incessantly deferred, in matters of their taste and style, to the judgment of the public frequenting Parisian Salons of painting, sculpture, drawing and engraving; that trusted in the experience of connoisseurs, collectors, and art critics who flocked to these venues. Together, these individuals formed a community of poets accustomed to visiting studios, all of whom were to a greater or lesser degree equipped with feelers that, while not driven by self-interest, were the most seasoned and daring artistic sensors of the world.

Le grand et sage écrivain, collectionneur averti à ses heures, serait bien surpris de découvrir à Paris aujourd'hui une FIAC annuelle qui se bat en vain et sottement, dans le plus beau cadre urbain du monde, pour concurrencer les Foires vedettes de l'économie mondialisée, Art Basel, Frieze London, etc., au lieu d'en prendre le contrepied.

Pardonnez-moi, mais de mon point de vue, cet échec est tout à l'honneur d'une capitale et d'une nation qui depuis quatre siècles (on pourrait remonter bien plus haut), ont pris sans discontinuer, pour arbitres de leur goût et de leurs styles, le public de leurs Salons de peinture, sculpture, dessin et gravure, connaisseurs, amateurs, critiques d'art - poètes habitués des ateliers, tous plus ou moins doués d'antennes désintéressées, les plus expérimentées et hardies du monde.

Chapter 3

The anthropology and sociology of the arts suggested by the Abbé Du Bos – and to which Voltaire unreservedly subscribed – take us back to Ciceronian, Virgilian, and Horatian rhetoric and poetics, transposed to Paris and into the French language. French, as a metalanguage,[35] escaped dogmatism and pedantism for a long time, and enjoyed the almost unconditional support, in the eighteenth century, of the courts of Europe. If French rhetoric and poetics required some philosophy, it is an eclectic philosophy, conciliatory but hostile to any systematization; one in which the Platonism of the New Academy balances the idealism of the Old Academy with its own skepticism and Epicureanism. This eclecticism is perfectly adjusted to capture the facets of the sensible and fantastic experience of the Beautiful. The plausible and convincing representation of human actions and passions that painting and poetry can accomplish falls under the Greek term *eïkos* (in Latin, *verisimilitude*); the agreeable and coherent organization of the plot pertains to the Greek term *prepon* (in Latin,

III

L'anthropologie et la sociologie des arts suggérées par l'abbé Du Bos, et que Voltaire endosse sans réserve, renvoient à une rhétorique et une poétique cicéroniennes, virgiliennes et horatiennes transportées en français à Paris. Ce métalangage, qui échappe au dogmatisme et au pédantisme, a bénéficié longtemps, au XVIIIe siècle, du consensus quasi unanime des cours européennes. Si cette rhétorique et cette poétique impliquent quelque philosophie, c'est une philosophie éclectique, conciliatrice, hostile à tout système et où le platonisme de la Nouvelle Académie pondère de scepticisme et d'épicurisme l'idéalisme de l'Ancienne Académie. Cet éclectisme convient parfaitement à rendre compte des facettes de l'expérience sensible et imaginative du beau. Les représentations probables et vraisemblables des actions et des passions humaines que proposent peinture et poésie relèvent de l'*eïkos* grec, [la *verisimilitudo* latine] ; l'enchaînement convenable et cohérent de leur récit relèvent du *prepon* grec [le *decor* latin] et le sens de la surprise et des

decor); the element of surprise and unpredictable coincidences enters into the category of the Greek *kaïros*. This last notion, paradigm for the impossibility to translate the Greek notion of discontinuous time, could find its Latin equivalent in *faustus*, and, as imperfectly, in the French expression *l'instant propice* (the serendipitous moment).

Nothing could be further removed from this "improvised tinkering," or bricolage (to borrow once again this metaphor introduced by Claude Lévi-Strauss) than the *episteme*[36] of Cartesian or empiricist sciences; but nothing could be closer to the trivial and brief experience of a lifespan and to the oratory and dialogical practice of surmising, the *doxa*. When this "improvised tinkering" (*bricolage*) is applied to poetry or the imitating arts, it no longer assigns them as central mission to teach (*docere*), but to please (*delectare*) and to move emotionally (*movere, flectere*). All of these rhetorical notions lack analytical precision, of which science and philosophy pride themselves. Their skepticism with respect to reason's ability to explain the arts culminated by the seventeenth century in the preterition[37] of the "I don't know what" – or, in French, "Je ne sais quoi."

However, it is precisely the shortcomings of the rheto-poetical language, which prevent it from imposing on the arts and letters an oppressive and sterilizing regularity, while endowing them with a fluid and subtle reflexivity that prevent them from falling for the shoddy unfinishedness of subjectivism and aesthetic relativism.

As much as he may have come across as a "modern" during the Quarrel between the Ancients and the Moderns,[38] Fontenelle, perpetual secretary of the Academy of Sciences, concurred with Boileau and Du Bos in the following respect: "Speculations about the nature of rules do not bestow genius on those who are lacking them; rules do not help very much either

imprévisibles conjonctures relèvent du *kaïros* grec. Cette notion grecque du temps discontinu, l'intraduisible par excellence, pourrait trouver un équivalent latin qui serait *faustus* et, en français, tout aussi imparfait, *l'instant propice.*

Rien de plus étranger que ce « bricolage » (pour emprunter encore une fois cette métaphore à Claude Lévi-Strauss), à l'épistémé de la science cartésienne ou de la science empiriste, mais rien de plus familier à l'expérience commune et quotidienne de la vie brève dans le temps et à l'exercice oratoire ou dialogique du vraisemblable, de la *doxa.* Lorsque ce bricolage s'applique à la poésie et aux arts d'imitation, il ne leur donne plus pour fin majeure le *docere*, mais le plaire (*delectare*) et l'émouvoir (*movere, flectere*). Toutes ces notions rhétoriques manquent de la précision analytique dont se prévalent la science et la philosophie. Leur scepticisme envers la capacité de la raison à expliquer les arts culmine au XVIIe siècle dans la prétérition du « Je ne sais quoi ».

Or ce sont justement les défauts de ce langage rhéto-poétique qui l'empêchent d'imposer aux arts et aux lettres une régularité oppressive et stérilisante, tout en les pourvoyant d'une réflexivité fluide et souple qui les retient de tomber dans le mauvais infini du subjectivisme et le relativisme esthétiques.

Tout « Moderne » qu'il fût dans la Querelle, Fontenelle, secrétaire perpétuel de l'Académie des sciences a pu écrire dans le même sens que Boileau et Du Bos : « Les spéculations sur la nature des règles ne donnent point de génie à ceux qui en manquent ; elles n'aident pas beaucoup à ceux qui en ont, et le plus souvent même les gens de génie sont incapables d'être aidés par les spéculations. À quoi donc sont-elles bonnes ? À faire remonter, jusqu'aux premières idées du beau, quelques gens qui aiment le raisonnement, et qui se plaisent à réduire sous l'empire de la philosophie les choses qui en paraissent les plus

those who follow them, and most frequently individuals of genius draw no benefits from speculation. For what is speculation therefore good? It helps some people who like reasoning go back to primordial ideas of the Beautiful; these are the people who enjoy reducing, under the pretext of philosophy, things which seem furthest removed from thought [for example, art], and which are commonly believed to follow the eccentricities of taste" (***Œuvres***, 1754, pp. 375-76, cit. Saisselin, p. 127). Even though, over the course of the eighteenth century, the circle of art authorities expanded from artists and *amateurs* of the Academy to Salon critics,[39] the language of this extended circle of discussants remained constraint to the oratory topos. This moderation was the subject of a consensus to which even the French philosophers of the Beautiful subscribed, and from which deviated neither the Jesuit Father Yves-Marie André, in his ***Essay on the Beautiful*** (***Essai du Beau***), published in 1741, nor the Abbé Charles Batteux, in his 1746 treatise entitled ***The Fine Arts Reduced to One Same Principle*** (***Les Baux-arts réduits à un même principe***).

Very modest in his ambitions, the Cartesian and Malbranchiste[40] Father André advanced a divine Idea of the Beautiful inaccessible from the here and now, except for in the perception of a rainbow, epitome of Beauty apprehensible through the senses, the nuances of which, in all their classifications and descriptions, take up most of the space in his book. As for the Abbé Batteux, a famous rhetorician who taught at the Collège de France and who was elected in this capacity to the Academy of Inscriptions (1754), and then to the French Academy, he piped in with Abbé Du Bos' language. He helped himself to the same Ciceronian and Quintilian vocabulary as could be found in the speeches that artists and *amateurs* delivered before the Academy of Painting. "Taste in the arts," he wrote, "is the same as intelligence in the sciences." And furthermore, "taste must be a sentiment that

indépendantes et que l'on croit communément abandonnées à la bizarrerie des goûts » (***Œuvres***, 1754, p. 375-276, cit. Saisselin, p. 127). Même si au cours du XVIIIe siècle le cercle des autorités sur les arts s'élargit des artistes et des amateurs de l'Académie à la critique des Salons, le langage de cette large conversation reste circonscrit à la topique oratoire. Cette modération fait l'objet d'un consensus dont même les « philosophes » français du Beau, tel le Père jésuite Yves-Marie André, dans son ***Essai sur le Beau*** publié en 1741, ou l'abbé Charles Batteux, dans son traité intitulé ***Les Beaux-arts réduits à un même principe***, publié en 1746, ne se sont pas départis.

Très modeste dans son ambition, le cartésien et malebranchiste Père André suppose une Idée divine du Beau inaccessible ici bas, sinon dans la perception d'un arc en ciel de beautés sensibles et de leurs nuances dont le classement et la description occupent l'essentiel de son livre. Quant à l'abbé Batteux, célèbre rhétoricien qui enseigna cet art au Collège de France, et qui fut élu à ce titre à l'Académie des Inscriptions (1754), puis à l'Académie française (1761), il est au diapason du langage de l'abbé Du Bos. Il recourt au même vocabulaire cicéronien et quintilianiste qu'artistes et amateurs tiennent dans les conférences de l'Académie de peinture : « Le goût, écrit-il, est dans les arts ce que l'intelligence est dans les sciences » ou encore « Le goût doit être un sentiment qui nous avertit si la belle Nature est bien ou mal imitée ». Il est si peu disposé à remonter plus loin dans les racines du jugement de goût qu'il peut écrire : « Je laisse à la Métaphysique profonde à débrouiller tous les ressorts secrets de notre âme et à creuser les principes de ses opérations. Je n'ai pas besoin d'entrer dans ces discussions spéculatives où l'on est aussi obscur que sublime ».

Ce défi lancé par le célèbre Batteux à la philosophie sensualiste anglaise de Locke et à la philosophie idéaliste allemande de Wolff, sera bientôt relevé par l'Anglais Edmund Burke

tells us whether the imitation of Nature was well done or badly butchered." He was so uninterested in the roots of the judgment about taste that he did not shy from writing: "I will leave it to the profundity of Metaphysics[41] to sort out the most secret motivations of our soul and to dig into the principles of its workings. I find no need to enter into these speculative discussions, where one's talk becomes as obscure as it becomes sublime."

The challenge launched by the famous Batteux against Locke's British sensualist and Wolff's idealist German philosophy will soon be answered by the British Edmund Burke and the Germans Lessing, Baumgarten, and Kant – the fathers of philosophical Aesthetics. In France, even the *philosophes*[42] who compiled the ***Encyclopédie***, following the tracks of their leader Voltaire, carefully avoided to break away from Aristotelian-Ciceronian language, which had triumphed so brilliantly in the French fine arts and letters. Theoretical without ever losing sight of practical aspects and of reality, this non-systematic, non-dogmatic language, and its attending rhetoric guided by moderation, made Paris, in the age of Louis XIV and Louis XV, the capital of classicism – an intersection for a wide range of national schools and minds. D'Alembert, in a ***Dialogue between Poetry and Philosophy*** (***Dialogue entre la poésie et la philosophie***), published in Berlin in 1753, makes philosophy subscribe to Horace's famous saying *Omne tulit punctum qui miscuit utile dulci* (*He who mingles the useful with the sweet carries away the prize* [of the opportune or supreme moment of the *kaïros*]). The saying represents an application of the three objectives of oratory art to poetry and painting: to combine the useful aspect of instruction, *docere*, with *movere* and *delectare*, that is sweet pleasure.

The mathematician inside d'Alembert revealed himself to be a great rhetorician, when he demanded that novelty reinvigorate the "sweetness" of poetry and the arts. He

et par les Allemands Lessing, Baumgarten, et Kant, les pères de l'Esthétique philosophique. En France même les « philosophes » qui président à l'***Encyclopédie***, se sont bien gardés, dans le sillage de leur patron Voltaire, de sortir du langage aristotélicien-cicéronien qui avait si bien réussi aux beaux arts et aux belles lettres françaises. C'était ce langage non systématique, non dogmatique, théorique sans jamais perdre de vue la pratique et le réel, en d'autres termes une rhétorique imprégnée de mesure, qui avait fait de Paris sous Louis XIV et Louis XV la capitale du classicisme européen, au carrefour de la diversité de ses écoles et de ses esprits nationaux. D'Alembert, dans un ***Dialogue entre la poésie et la philosophie*** publié à Berlin en 1753, fait agréer par la philosophie le fameux apophtegme d'Horace, *Omne tulit punctum qui miscuit utile dulci* (« Il a touché entièrement juste [c'est le ***kaïros***] celui qui a su mêler le doux à l'utile »), application à la poésie et à la peinture des trois objectifs de l'art oratoire : mêler au *docere,* l'utile, le *movere* et le *delectare*, le doux.

D'Alembert le mathématicien se révèle excellent rhéteur, quand il demande que la nouveauté renouvelle la « douceur » de la poésie et des arts. Il entend par nouveauté celle de l'expression, que Cicéron, dans l'*Orator,* décrit en ces termes : « On suppose nouvelles dans mes ouvrages des choses très anciennes, mais trop peu connues ».

Mais le cas le plus typique, c'est celui de Diderot, qui en 1751 écrit en métaphysicien des ***Recherches philosophiques sur l'origine et la nature du Beau***, qu'il publiera l'année suivante dans l'entrée « Beau » de ***L'Encyclopédie.*** Il y concluait que, dans tous les domaines où le beau se manifeste, il consiste en la perception d'un rapport entre le perçu et le percevant. Du fait qu'il ne renvoie pas à un Beau absolu, le beau perçu est tenu pour aussi peu définissable que le goût, notoirement inconstant et capricieux. Diderot ne s'en tint pas à cette idée générale et banale. À partir de 1759 jusqu'en 1763, Diderot,

understood novelty as an expression analogous to what Cicero described as follows in the *Orator*: "In my works, one can interpret novelty to mean very ancient things that are but too little known."

But the most consequential case is that of Diderot. It was Diderot, who, in 1751, wrote as metaphysician the ***Philosophical Researches into the Origins and the Nature of Beauty*** (***Recherches philosophiques sur l'origine et la nature du Beau***), which he published in the following year as the dictionary entry under the heading "Beauty" in the *Encyclopédie*. He concluded that in all the areas where the beautiful manifests itself, it consists of an awareness for the relationship between that which is perceived and the one who is perceiving. Given that he does claim to be the purveyor of an absolute notion of Beauty, the beautiful perceived is held to be as impossible to define as taste, itself notorious for being inconsistent and capricious. From 1759 through 1763, Diderot, in order to keep up to date with the chronicle of the "Salons" in his ***Correspondance littéraire***,[43] imposes himself a true artistic re-education program. He frequents the studios of great artists, such as Chardin, La Tour, and Falconet.

He familiarizes himself with their working methods, their problems, their language. Lacking the pedigree of an *amateur*, understood in the sense of an erudite and refined art collector like the Count de Caylus or Mariette, but having been trained all his life in the arts, Diderot became an eloquent art critic. He invested his determination to share his pleasures or displeasures inspired by the paintings in the Salon with his virtuosity as rhetorician and all of his talent as an actor. When writing about the Salon of 1765, he infused the antique saying by Horace, *ut pictura poesis*, with new life for the princely subscribers of the ***Correspondance***. To this end, he did not hesitate to present himself as a latter-day Philostratus:

afin de tenir en connaissance de cause sa chronique des « Salons » de la ***Correspondance littéraire***, s'impose une véritable rééducation artistique. Il fréquente les ateliers de grands artistes, Chardin, La Tour, Falconet.

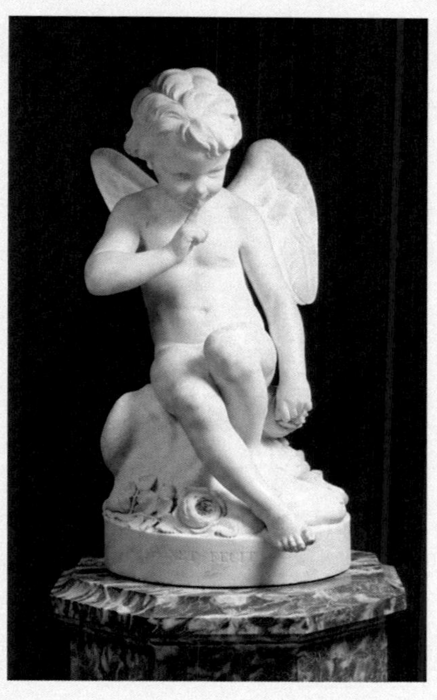

Étienne Falconet, ***Menacing Cupid*** (***L'Amour menaçant***), 1757, marble, 36 in. x 19 3/4 in. x 24 1/2 in. (91.5 x 50 x 62 cm). Louvre, Paris, RF296.

Il s'initie à leur pratique, à leurs problèmes, à leur langage. Sans pouvoir être qualifié d'amateur, au sens érudit et raffiné d'un Caylus ou d'un Mariette, entraînés toute une vie aux arts, Diderot se fait éloquent critique d'art. Il met toute sa virtuosité de rhéteur et tout son talent d'acteur à faire partager le plaisir ou le déplaisir que lui inspirent les tableaux du Salon. Dans celui de 1765, illustrant l'antique apophtegme horatien *ut pictura poesis* et s'adressant aux abonnés princiers de la ***Correspondance,*** il n'hésite pas à se donner pour le moderne Philostrate :

« Je vous décrirai les tableaux, et ma description sera telle qu'avec un peu d'imagination et de goût on les réalisera dans l'espace et qu'on y posera les objets à peu près comme nous les avons vus sur la toile. »

À la rhétorique en tant que langage réflexif (ou métalangage) du procès d'invention de

"I will describe paintings to you, and my description will be such that with a small amount of imagination and taste, you can recreate them in space and introduce, one by one, objects such as I have seen them on the real canvas."

Diderot added to the reflective language (or metalanguage) engaging the artwork's creative genesis another rhetorical level, customized for the recipients of his Salon criticism, who resided far away from Paris. This is a receptive, mediating, and appreciative rhetoric evolving around the artworks on display, which the critic had all the time to see, admire, or detest, sparing his correspondents the trouble of a long travel. The geographically distant reader must contend himself with retaining only the conclusions of Diderot's discourse and the retracing of the critic's footsteps. In this other rhetoric, where Diderot revealed himself to be an inventive orator-actor-improviser, the reader never loses sight of the work of art, and, by extension, shares in the author's mimetic and erotic proprieties or improprieties.

Rediscovered at the beginning of the Bourbon Restauration (1814-1830), Diderot's art criticism inspired one of the great literary genres of Romanticism, handed down with renewed genius from one generation of art writers to the next, from Stendhal, Balzac, Gautier, to the Goncourt brothers, Baudelaire, Fénéon, Mirbeau, and Proust.[44]

This French fidelity to rhetorical metalanguages and to the reversibility of verbal and non-verbal painting, which marked the success of French art since the reign of Louis XIII, can no longer be taken for granted in 1750s Europe. It is strongly called into question in England and Germany. In 1750, Alexander Baumgarten published the first part of his ***Aesthetica***, the treatise of a new philosophical discipline which he was the first to name. He pretended that aesthetics would replace, one step

l'œuvre d'art, correspond une autre rhétorique à l'intention des destinataires absents du Salon, une rhétorique réceptrice, médiatrice et appréciative des œuvres que le critique d'art a eu tout le temps de voir, de comparer, d'admirer ou de détester, épargnant à ses correspondants le soin de se déplacer. Le lecteur lointain peut se contenter de ne retenir que les conclusions du discours et du parcours du critique. Dans cette autre rhétorique où Diderot se révèle un inventif orateur-acteur-improvisateur, on ne perd pas de vue l'œuvre d'art, et par procuration, on éprouve ses propriétés ou impropriétés mimétiques et érotiques.

Redécouvert au début de la Restauration, Diderot critique d'art inspirera l'un des grands genres littéraires du romantisme, pratiqué avec un génie renouvelé de génération en génération, par Stendhal, Balzac, Gautier, les Goncourt, Baudelaire, Fénéon, Mirbeau, Proust.

Cette fidélité française au métalangage rhétorique et à cette réversibilité des peintures verbales et non verbales, qui avait fait le succès des arts français depuis le règne de Louis XIII, ne va plus de soi en Europe dans les années 1750. Elle est vivement remise en cause en Angleterre et en Allemagne. En 1750, Alexander Baumgarten publie la première partie de son ***Aesthetica***, discipline philosophique nouvelle qu'il est le premier à nommer, et où il prétend substituer aux à peu près de la théorie française des arts la rigueur systématique de son maître, Christian Wolff. En 1757, au nom de la Bible, de Shakespeare, et de Milton, et sur les traces de l'épistémologie sensualiste lockienne, la boussole de la rhéto-poétique française, le *decor*, [la *convenientia*, le *prépon*], est pulvérisée par Edmund Burke, dans sa ***Recherche philosophique sur l'origine de nos idées du sublime et du beau.*** Le jeune philosophe anglais construit le Beau et le Sublime, qui jusqu'alors n'étaient que deux modes rhétoriques du grand style, en deux concepts résolument antithétiques. Implicitement,

at a time, French art theory with the systematic rigor of his master, Christian Wolff. Seven years later, Edmund Burke published ***A Philosophical Enquiry into the Origin of Our Ideas of the Sublime and the Beautiful***. Wandering on the tracks of Lockian sensualist epistemology,[45] he broke, in the name of the Bible, Shakespeare, and Milton, the French rheto-poetic compass of *decor* [in the sense of *convenientia*, or *prepon*; English: decorum]. The young philosopher separated the Beautiful and the Sublime, until then but two rhetorical modes of the grand style, into two resolutely antithetical subjects. Implicitly, he associated French taste, designed to absorb and to calm disquietude, with the Beautiful, while the King James Bible, Shakespeare, and Milton, which incite the nervous system, fell under the category of the Sublime. In 1764, it was the turn of the German Johannes Joachim Winckelmann, known for his francophobe attitude, to interpret the history of art in terms of conceptual aesthetics. He elevated Greek art of the 5th century to the model of absolute Beauty – without precedent and without successor, especially when compared to classical art from the century of Louis XIV.

Two years later, another great German mind, Gotthold Ephraim Lessing, in his ***Laocoön***, tackled the motto *Ut pictura poesis*, the keystone of the French classical edifice. He countered the saying with the radical antithesis between Poetry and Painting-Sculpture, declaring the first a temporal art, and the two others spatial arts, and as such incompatible with each other.

Nevertheless, as we saw, this vigorous anglo-germanic assault on Paris, capital of the arts, did not get anybody upset in France, except Voltaire, who lashed out against the very same Shakespeare, whom, in 1734, he had imprudently introduced to the French people in his ***Philosophical Letters*** (***Lettres philosophiques***). Even the word aesthetics was

il identifie le goût français, qui vise à occuper et calmer l'inquiétude, dans la catégorie du Beau, alors que la King James Bible, Shakespeare et Milton, qui font chavirer le système nerveux, relèvent de la catégorie du Sublime. En 1764, c'est au tour de l'Allemand Johannes Joachim Winckelmann, très francophobe, de traiter l'histoire de l'art en esthéticien conceptuel. Il pose l'art grec du Ve siècle en modèle du Beau absolu, sans précédent, sans successeur, même et surtout chez les classiques du Grand siècle français.

Deux ans plus tard, un autre grand esprit allemand, Gotthold Ephraïm Lessing, s'en prend dans son ***Laocoön*** à l'apothtegme ***Ut pictura poesis***, la clef de voûte de l'édifice du classicisme français. Il lui oppose l'antithèse radicale entre Poésie et Peinture-Sculpture, décrétée l'une, art du temps, les deux autres, arts de l'espace, et comme tels insuperposables.

Pour autant, nous l'avons vu, ce vigoureux assaut anglo-allemand contre Paris capitale des arts n'émut personne en France, sauf Voltaire, qui se déchaîna contre le même Shakespeare qu'il avait eu l'imprudence de faire connaître aux Français en 1734 dans ses ***Lettres philosophiques.*** Le mot même d'esthétique n'entra pas dans la langue avant les années 1850. La nouvelle discipline introduite en 1750 par Baumgarten et reconfigurée par Kant en 1790, dans sa *Critique de la faculté de juger*, n'entra dans l'enseignement français qu'au XXe siècle, mais elle a largement pris sa revanche depuis, même dans les Écoles des Beaux-arts.

Le peintre Amaury Duval, élève de David et grand ami d'Ingres, écrivait, en 1801 à propos de Kant et de la troisième ***Critique*** : « Les Français ne voudront pas le croire, mais le Platon de l'Allemagne vient de prouver que c'est par instinct plutôt que par raisonnement qu'ils ont eu jusqu'à présent quelques succès dans les beaux arts [...]. Nous nous empressons de recueillir avec respect et reconnaissance les

not part of anybody's French vocabulary before the 1850s. The new discipline introduced in 1750 by Baumgarten and reconfigured by Kant's ***Critique of the Power of Judgment*** in 1790, did not become part of French education until the twentieth century, but has since had its day of revenge, even in art schools.

The painter Amaury-Duval, a student of David and a close friend of Ingres, commented, in 1801, Kant's third ***Critique*** as follows: "The French will not believe this, but Germany's Plato[46] has just demonstrated that it is by instinct rather than by reason that they [the French] had until now some success in the fine arts [...]. We hurry to receive with respect and gratitude the sublime principals of this scholar so celebrated by the universities on the other side of the Rhine. Kant will dethrone Locke and Condillac one day with much more success than Mercier [...]. It is possible that the ignorant mass of readers will not understand this sublime fragment of *Transcendental Philosophy* [previously cited by Amaury-Duval in Charles de Villers' translation]. We recommend that they read it one more time, and another time, until they understand. And then they can go visit our picture galleries and our schools to judge what constitutes the *truly beautiful*. Let us commiserate the poor Abbé Du Bos, who wrote three large volumes to teach a system that Kant's club reduced to dust."

The contributors to the periodical ***The Decade*** (***La Décade***), who informed Stendhal's thought, recycled Amaury-Duval's arguments against Germanic metaphysics. "All the aesthetics in the world," wrote one of them, "do not lead to the creation of a single masterwork, and are not worth one either." "Research on beauty, as happy an occupation one imagines it to be," wrote another, "is not worth a single artwork conceived from beauty. It is better to produce living beings than to dissect corpses." And again, "there is too much inequality between the artist or the poet

sublimes maximes de ce docteur si célèbre dans les universités d'Outre-Rhin, et qui doit un jour, avec plus de succès que Mercier, détrôner Locke et Condillac [...]. Il est possible que le vulgaire des lecteurs n'entende pas bien ce sublime fragment de la *Philosophie transcendantale* [qu'il vient de citer dans la traduction de Charles de Villers]. Nous leur conseillons de le lire une autre fois, une autre encore, enfin jusqu'à ce qu'il l'aient compris. Et alors ils pourront aller dans nos galeries de tableaux et dans nos lycées juger ce qui constitue le *vrai beau.* Plaignons le pauvre abbé Du Bos qui a fait trois gros volumes pour enseigner un système que la massue de Kant vient de réduire en poussière. »

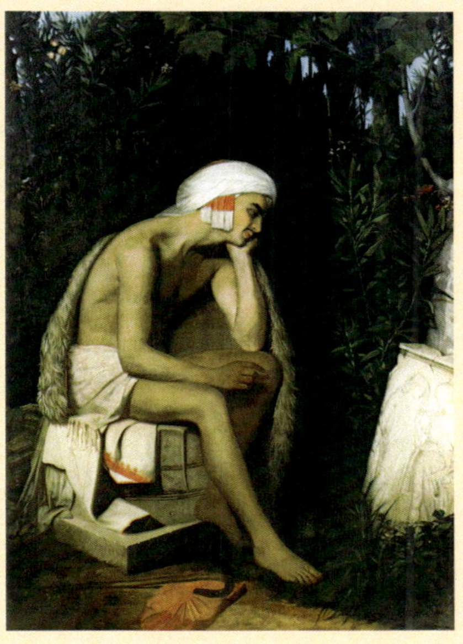

Eugène Emmanuel Amaury-Duval, ***The Greek Shepherd* (*Le Berger grec*)**, 1833, oil on canvas, 76 5/8 x 52 3/8 in. (187 x 133 cm). Private collection.

Les Idéologues de la revue ***La Décade***, les maîtres à penser de Stendhal, reprennent contre la métaphysique allemande les thèmes d'Amaury Duval, « Toute l'esthétique du monde, écrit l'un d'eux, ne fait pas un ouvrage de génie et ne le vaut pas ». « Des recherches sur le beau, quelque heureuses qu'on les imagine, ne valent pas, écrit un autre, une seule beauté de l'art ; il vaut mieux produire des êtres vivants que de les disséquer ». Ou encore : « Il y a trop d'inégalité

who produces and the critic who judges in order to put them on a level playing field."

Accustomed to a rhetorical language and its modest but time-honored approach towards the creation and the reception of a work of art, the French readers of Kant rejected a judgmental analysis of beauty, which, incidentally, denied beauty any other form of existence but that which is physically apparent. Before there emerged the great French school of art criticism, which I cited at the beginning of this essay – Gautier, the Goncourts, Baudelaire, and their likes – Germaine de Staël, in her influential book ***About Germany*** (***De l'Allemagne***), took sides, in 1810, with Abbé Du Bos and against the invasion of Europe's fine arts by the metaphysical language of Aesthetics:

"In [Schiller's] essay on grace and dignity and in his letter on Aesthetics, that is to say the theory of Beauty, one finds too much metaphysics. If one wants to speak about the enjoyment of the arts, to which all human beings are susceptible, it is better to always rely on received impressions, rather than to indulge in abstract forms that make one loose track of these impressions."

She also advocated, as an antidote against philosophical abstraction, the continuation of rhetorical art criticism, reinvented in Paris in the context of the Salons, and carried to new heights by Diderot:

"The lively description of masterworks," she wrote, "is a much stronger inspiration for criticism than general ideas floating about subjects without defining any of them."

The circle is closing, and the opinion that Mme de de Staël expressed in 1810 on the Germanic Aesthetics of Kant and Schiller, echoed directly, only with different words, that of Paul Valéry in 1937:

"The Aesthetics of the Metaphysicians demanded that one separate *Beauty* from *beautiful things*."

entre l'artiste, le poète qui produit et le critique qui juge, pour les mettre entre parallèle ».

Accoutumés à la rhétorique et à son attitude modestement, mais résolument prescriptive envers l'invention et la réception de l'œuvre d'art, les lecteurs français de Kant se refusent à une analyse du jugement sur le beau qui, par ailleurs, dénie au beau toute autre existence objective que l'apparence. Et avant que ne surgisse la grande école française de critique d'art par où j'ai commencé cet essai, les Gautier, les Goncourt, les Baudelaire, Germaine de Staël, dans son grand livre *De l'Allemagne*, prenait parti en 1810 pour l'abbé Du Bos et contre l'invasion des beaux-arts européens par le langage métaphysique de l'Esthétique:

« Dans l'essai [de Schiller] sur *la Grâce et la Dignité*, et dans ses Lettres sur l'*Esthétique*, c'est-à-dire la théorie du Beau, il y a trop de métaphysique. Lorsqu'on veut parler des jouissances des arts, dont tous les hommes sont susceptibles, il faut s'appuyer toujours sur les impressions qu'ils ont reçues et ne pas se permettre les formes abstraites qui font perdre la trace de ces impressions ».

Aussi préconise-t-elle contre l'abstraction philosophique, la perpétuation de la critique d'art rhétorique, réinventée à Paris, à l'occasion des Salons et portée très haut par Diderot :

« La description animée des chefs-d'œuvre, écrit-elle, donne bien plus d'intérêt à la critique que les idées générales qui planent sur tous les sujets, sans en caractériser aucun. »

Le cercle se referme, et l'opinion que Mme de Staël énonce, avec d'autres mots, en 1810, sur l'Esthétique allemande de Kant et de Schiller, rejoint exactement celle que prononcera Paul Valéry en 1937 :

« L'Esthétique des métaphysiciens exigeait que l'on séparât le *Beau* des *belles choses*. »

Endnotes

1. Étienne Delécluze, *Louis David: Son École et son temps* (Paris: Didier, 1855), 132-33: "Mengs, dont il ne goûta jamais le talent, et encore moins des philologues antiquaires, dont il ne connaissait guère les écrits que par le titre et par les gravures qu'ils renferment."

2. Bernard Berenson, *Seeing and Knowing* (New York: Macmillan, 1953), 3-4.

3. Implied reference to the "generation of 1968," whose intellectual leaders, especially in France, often claimed Maoism as an ideological model, understood as an umbrella term for a wide variety of ill-defined anarchist and communist currents at the time.

4. Reference to the German philosopher Georg Friedrich Hegel (1770-1831).

5. Latin, literally: "As is painting so is poetry." Horace's saying has often been interpreted to mean that poetry is like painting.

6. Andy Warhol famously bought Brillo boxes in the supermarket, signed them, and sold the "artwork" thus created in galleries. In the process, the Brillo box became synonymous with Warhol's Pop Art. By doing so, Marchel Duchamp recycled ideas pioneered during the first of half the twentieth century with his readymades.

7. Jean-Baptiste-Siméon Chardin (1699-1779), French painter best known for his small-format, meticulously rendered still lifes and portraits of children.

8. Nineteenth-century painters Both Corot, who was patronized by Napoleon III, and Manet, who was maligned by the art public, anticipated the arrival of Impressionism. Degas was a member of the Impressionist group of painters, founded in 1874.

9. Central building, now used by museums, on the fairground of former Parisian World Fairs. The current Palais de Chaillot, erected in 1937 in the Art Déco style, is adorned with Valéry's inscriptions.

10. "Will to power" is a key concept in the philosophy of Friedrich Nietzsche (1844-1900).

11. Reference to French mathematician and philosopher René Descartes (1596-1650; adj.: Cartesian), famous for the expression *cogito ergo sum*, "I think, therefore I am," and his mechanistic understanding of mind, nature, and the universe.

12. Figure of speech in which the whole is put for a part, part for whole, as in the expression "fifty hands," meaning "fifty men."

13. Seventeenth-century French playwrights, who often situated their plots in classical antiquity. See Borgehoff, *Freedom of French Classics* (1951).

14. In its original form, the *Encyclopédie* (*Encyclopedia*) was published between 1751 and 1772 in twenty-eight volumes, containing over 70,000 articles and more than 3,000 illustrations. Its general editors, Denis Diderot and Jean le Rond d'Alembert, recruited a corps of contributors that comprised some of the greatest Enlightenment thinkers, such as Montesquieu, Jean-Jacques Rousseau, Voltaire, or the Baron d'Holbach. Each author was responsible for writing the entries that fell within his particular field of expertise. Its secular, scientific outlook and implicit belief that all knowledge is finite made the *Encyclopédie* one of the outstanding accomplishment of the Enlightenment.

15. Written by the Greek philosopher Plato in about 380 B.C.E., the *Republic* represents perhaps the first attempt to develop a theoretical blueprint for what an ideal society should look like.

16. Gotthold Ephraim Lessing (1729-1781) opened his treatise *Laocoön*, so named in reference to the famous Hellenistic sculpture group and its textural roots in Vergil's *Aenead*, with a discussion of Horace's saying *Ut pictura poesis*. He rejects Horace's core message that painting and poetry are intrinsically related.

17. Mnemotechnical: aiding the memory; apothegm: a short saying.

18. In ancient Greece, a description of images, especially in a rhetorical context.

19. In his *Iliad*, Homer provided a description of the pictorial elements found on Achilles' (legendary) shield.

20. French authors and art critics of the eighteenth (Diderot) and nineteenth (Gautier, Goncourts) centuries.

21. Heyday of the Baroque period, embodied by artists like Bernini and Caravaggio. Important artistic and architectural additions were made to the Vatican during this era.

22. Conversation partner.

23. Art Expert; literally: someone who understands/listens to the arts.

24. French seventeenth-century painter active for most of his life in Rome and best known for his mythological scenes of vaguely classical inspiration. In 1740, he received a summons by Louis XIII to return to France, but before long he was back in Rome. Poussin became a role model for eighteenth-century French neoclassical painters, especially Jacques-Louis David and his students.

25. The term *amateur* mostly refers to knowledgeable art collectors and, in a larger sense, to anybody who can write competently about art without producing art himself. Soon after its foundation, the French Academy of Painting and Sculpture began to admit *amateurs*.

26. Shortly before his own death, in 1715, Louis XV had lost most of his children and grandchildren, leaving the succession of the Sun King unresolved. Since his surviving great-grandson was still a minor, a distant relative from the Orléans line stepped in as a Regent until Louis XV would reach maturity. The period of the Duc d'Orléans' interim rule, 1715-1723, is called the Regency.

27. Reference to a quarrel among painters and *amateurs* in the Academy at the turn of the eighteenth century. The "colorists" were followers of Peter Paul Rubens, who were opposed by those who subscribed to the emphasis on line drawing, embodied by the art of Nicolas Poussin (1594-1665).

28. Reference to Blaise Pascal (1623-1662), French mathematician, physicist and philosopher.

29. Philosophy stressing the enjoyment of sensual pleasures (f. ex. good food) and the absence of suffering to create a state of happiness, named after early fourth-century B.C.E. philosopher Epicurus.

30. The full Latin quote reads in translation, "it is pleasant, when the winds are buffeting the waves on the great sea, to watch from the land the great struggle of another," which is frequently interpreted as an expression of the comfort found in the truth of philosophy (as opposed to those "struggling" souls who neither seek nor find it).

31. "Each one is drawn by his own delight."

32. The "sounder part"; for instance, in an electoral assembly.

33. Pleasure of the word.

34. Louis XIV, late in his rule, started several wars and left state finances in disarray. Ill and bedridden, the king became morose and increasingly pious in his old age.

35. Language and (cultural) symbols used to investigate matters pertaining to language itself.

36. Although of Greek derivation (Gr. "espistemai": to understand, to know for certain, to believe), the expression *episteme* is closely associated with the French philosopher and sociologist Michel Foucault (1926-1984). It designates figures of speech or institutions, which are generally held to be true and universal, but may not be so.

37. That which is passed by or left out (especially in speech).

38. Famous intellectual controversy in France, which reached its peak around 1690, dealing with the issue whether classical antiquity or modern-day ingenuity should be the guiding light of human culture and civilization.

39. Salons: Official art exhibitions organized by the French Academy of Painting and Sculpture since the 17th century. Salon critics were art critics who wrote about the art on display in the Salons; the first critics (La Font de Saint-Yenne, Diderot, etc.) emerged in the 18th century.

40. Reference to Nicolas Malbranche (1638-1715), a French rhetorician and philosopher.

41. The term metaphysics, here and in other places of Prof. Fumaroli's speech, must be largely defined to allude to thought models and philosophies that are overly and unnecessarily convoluted or abstract. Originally, the term pertained to that branch of philosophy which deals with the character, nature, causes, etc. of God; by extension it became an expression referring to any (pseudo-)science dealing with the supernatural or with magic.

42. Collectively, Enlightenment thinkers, many of whom contributed as authors to the *Encyclopédie*. See also note 14 above.

43. A newsletter, written by Diderot, that circulated in manuscript format in German and Eastern European courts about current cultural events in France (especially visual arts, literature, etc.).

44. Some of the most famous French nineteenth-century novelists and poets.

45. The branch of philosophy that is concerned with the question of how we know what we know.

46. Ironical swipe at Kant.